Fresh Ways with
Snacks and Canapés

COVER
Vivid colours and elegant shapes make these assorted canapés the culinary height of any party. Low-fat toppings such as fish mousse, asparagus tips, and breasts of chicken and duck are set on bread bases and contained in a shimmering layer of vegetable aspic.

TIME-LIFE BOOKS

EUROPEAN EDITOR: Ellen Phillips
Design Director: Ed Skyner
Director of Editorial Resources: Samantha Hill
Chief Sub-Editor: Ilse Gray

HOW THINGS WORK
SYSTEM EARTH
LIBRARY OF CURIOUS AND UNUSUAL FACTS
BUILDING BLOCKS
A CHILD'S FIRST LIBRARY OF LEARNING
VOYAGE THROUGH THE UNIVERSE
THE THIRD REICH
MYSTERIES OF THE UNKNOWN
TIME-LIFE HISTORY OF THE WORLD
FITNESS, HEALTH & NUTRITION
HEALTHY HOME COOKING
UNDERSTANDING COMPUTERS
THE ENCHANTED WORLD
LIBRARY OF NATIONS
PLANET EARTH
THE GOOD COOK
THE WORLD'S WILD PLACES

ISBN 0 7054 2013 2
TIME-LIFE is a trademark of Time Warner Inc. U.S.A.

HEALTHY HOME COOKING

Editorial Staff for *Fresh Ways with Snacks and Canapés*
SERIES EDITOR: Jackie Matthews
Researcher: Susie Dawson
Designers: Lynne Brown, Mike Snell
Sub-Editor: Wendy Gibbons
Studio Stylist: Liz Hodgson
Editorial Assistant: Eugénie Romer

Picture Department
Administrator: Patricia Murray
Picture Co-ordinator: Amanda Hindley

Editorial Production
Chief: Maureen Kelly
Assistant: Samantha Hill
Editorial Department: Theresa John, Debra Lelliott

THE CONTRIBUTORS

PAT ALBUREY is a home economist with a wide experience of preparing foods for photography, teaching cookery and creating recipes. She has written a number of cookery books and was the studio consultant for the Time-Life Series *The Good Cook*.

JOANNA BLYTHMAN is an amateur cook and recipe writer who owns a specialist food shop in Edinburgh. She contributes articles on cookery to a number of newspapers and trade periodicals.

SILVIJA DAVIDSON studied at Leith's School of Food and Wine and specializes in the development of recipes from Latvia and other international cuisines.

JANICE MURFITT trained as a home economist and worked as a cookery editor on *Family Circle* magazine. Her cookery book titles include *Cheesecakes and Flans*, *Entertaining Friends* and *Rice and Pasta*.

JEREMY ROUND, a former deputy editor of the *Good Food Guide*, is food correspondent of *The Independent* and the author of a book on Turkish regional cookery.

The following also contributed recipes to this volume:
Alexandra Carlier, Graeme Gore-Rowe, Yvonne Hamlett, Carole Handslip, Antony Kwok, Lynn Rutherford.

THE COOKS

The recipes in this book were cooked for photography by Pat Alburey, Jacki Baxter, Allyson Birch, Jill Eggleton, Joanna Farrow, Anne Gains, Carole Handslip, Antony Kwok, Dolly Meers, Janice Murfitt, Lesley Sandall, Michelle Thompson. *Studio Assistant:* Rita Walters

NUTRITION CONSULTANT

PATRICIA JUDD trained as a dietician and worked in hospital practice before returning to university to obtain her MSc and PhD degrees. Since then she has lectured in Nutrition and Dietetics at London University.

Nutritional analyses for *Fresh Ways with Snacks and Canapés* were derived from McCance and Widdowson's *The Composition of Food* by A. A. Paul and D. A. T. Southgate, and other current data.

This volume is one of a series of illustrated cookery books that emphasize the preparation of healthy dishes for today's weight-conscious, nutrition-minded eaters.

Fresh Ways with Snacks and Canapés

BY

THE EDITORS OF TIME-LIFE BOOKS

TIME-LIFE BOOKS/AMSTERDAM

Contents

Spiced Peanut Dip with Crudité Skewers

Green-Jacket Dublin Bay Prawns

Miniature Samosas

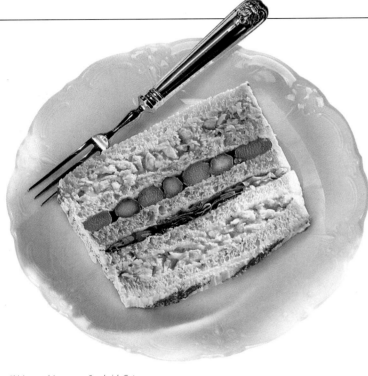

Chicken and Asparagus Sandwich Gateau

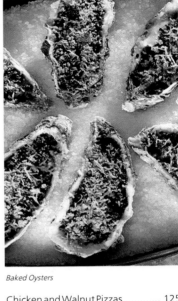

Baked Oysters

Goat Cheese on Toast

Hospitable Fare

Eating between meals, or relying on a snack to take the place of one, may come high on the list of nutritional sins. But from time to time most of us succumb to temptation or necessity. Visiting friends on the spur of the moment, or attending some special celebration, we are hard-pressed to refuse the refreshments that are offered: the sharing of food is, after all, the heart and soul of hospitality. Coming home late after an evening out, a full-scale dinner is often out of the question; instead, we content ourselves with a snack.

But sociable or casual eating does not need to be self-destructive. Food consumed between meals, or instead of them, can be light, wholesome, high in nutrients and low in those banes of the contemporary diet: saturated fats, sugar and excess salt. This volume presents a completely new approach to formal and informal entertaining, a world away from the usual assortment of fat-laden, over-salted crisps and nuts, thickly mayonnaised dips, and stodgy, high-calorie canapés. It provides a repertoire of welcoming food for all occasions, formal or informal, large or small, planned weeks in advance or conjured up as an impromptu treat.

The volume is divided into four chapters. The first two offer ideas for parties: Chapter 1 concentrates on cold party food, Chapter 2 on hot. Informal snacks, including sandwiches, are covered in the third chapter, while the final section of the book presents recipes uniquely suited to microwave cookery. All 126 recipes have been devised in accordance with contemporary nutritional thinking, emphasizing the use of fresh, natural ingredients, with minimal reliance on saturated fats and salt, and an avoidance, wherever possible, of processed foods.

Butter is used in small quantities, or replaced by polyunsaturated oils where appropriate, and low-fat yogurt is substituted for cream. Meat is scrupulously trimmed of fat; poultry likewise is freed of fat and skin. Much use is made of fresh vegetables and fruit; herbs and spices serve as natural sources of flavour; excessively rich, heavy sauces are abandoned in favour of light dressings and aromatic marinades.

Moderation, rather than rigid abstinence, is the governing principle. A certain amount of fat, for instance, is necessary to keep the human body in good working order, and to help transform the foods we eat into usable energy. But too much fat — particularly the saturated fats found in fatty meats and dairy products — is now generally believed to contribute to heart disease, obesity, digestive disorders and, according to recent research, to the development of certain cancers.

Ironically, the snacks that most people find hardest to resist, and easiest to consume far too many of, are those that are highest in fat content: savoury titbits such as potato crisps, corn chips and other items that derive their golden colour and eminently satisfying crunch from immersion in a pot of bubbling fat. Happily, there are also other ways to achieve a pleasurably crunchy texture. Grilling foods instead of deep frying them, or sautéing them in a small amount of an oil — such as safflower or sunflower — that is high in polyunsaturated fats, produces excellent results. Bite-sized savoury biscuits made from low-fat dough, flavoured with Parmesan cheese, sesame seeds or crushed garlic, are lighter and less cloying than the ubiquitous party snacks that are sold commercially in tins or packets; and lightly toasted chick-peas make a pleasant — and healthy — change from greasy salted nuts.

Salt too has been the subject of concern and controversy. Salt occurs naturally in many foods; it is a traditional and effective preservative, and a certain amount of salt is essential for good health. Yet practically everyone who eats a typical Western diet, and consumes any quantity of processed food, is consuming salt far in excess of their bodily needs. People with blood pressure problems, in particular, are often warned by their doctors to cut down on salt, or cut it out altogether. But an inspired use of other flavourings can render salt on snacks superfluous. Popcorn, for instance, here gains savour from a spicy tomato coating or from curry spices, while an easy recipe for home-made pretzels coats the twists in herbs instead of salt.

Favourites from around the world

All the world's cuisines lend fresh inspiration. From Spain comes a substantial omelette of peppers and potatoes that uses only half an egg per serving. India contributes samosas and koftas — pastry triangles enclosing a spicy filling and aromatic meatballs made with minced chicken. Provence supplies a vinaigrette-dressed salad in a sandwich, indispensable for picnics on the beach, and the French equivalent to the Italian pizza — *pissaladière*. Delicacies with a Middle Eastern influence range from a chick-pea and yogurt dip to the little cigar-shaped phyllo pastries known as *sigara borek*. Peru provides its own exotic, high-protein favourite — skewered morsels of chili-spiced ox heart that will tempt the most unadventurous of meat-eaters.

From China, which has elevated the between-meals snack into a national pastime, come sesame prawn toasts — made here without resorting to deep-fat frying — and seafood wontons, traditionally cooked in a bamboo steamer, although in this instance filled with a very European combination of fresh and smoked salmon. Japanese sushi, the elegant parcels of fresh fish, rice and seaweed, are presented along with some cosmopolitan variations on the theme: ruby-red radicchio leaves as wrappers, or slivers of red pepper, avocado and olives augmenting the traditional seafood filling.

The Key to Better Eating

Healthy Home Cooking addresses the concerns of today's weight-conscious, health-minded cooks with recipes that take into account guidelines set by nutritionists. The secret of eating well, of course, has to do with maintaining a balance of foods in the diet; most of us consume too much sugar and salt, too much fat and too many calories, even too much protein. In planning a snack, the recipes should be used thoughtfully in the context of a day's eating. To make the choice easier, this book presents an analysis of nutrients either in a single snack serving, as in the breakdown on the right, or per item. Where a dish includes a sauce or dip, the per item analysis includes a proportion of the sauce or dip. The cook should also bear in mind that moderation, as in all things, is a good policy to follow when seeking to prepare a balanced display.

Interpreting the chart

The chart below gives dietary guidelines for healthy men, women and children. Recommended figures vary from country to country, but the principles are the same everywhere. Here, the average daily amounts of calories and protein are from a report by the U.K. Department of Health and Social Security; the maximum advisable daily intake of fat is based on guidelines given by the National Advisory Committee on Nutrition Education (NACNE); those for cholesterol and sodium are based on upper limits suggested by the World Health Organization.

The volumes in the Healthy Home Cooking series do not purport to be diet books, nor do they focus on health foods. Rather, they express a commonsense approach to cooking that uses salt, sugar, cream, butter and oil in moderation while employing other ingredients that also provide flavour and satisfaction. Herbs, spices, aromatic vegetables, fruits and vinegars are all used to this end.

The recipes make few unusual demands. Naturally, they call for fresh ingredients,

---

Calories **180**
Protein **6g**
Cholesterol **70mg**
Total fat **8g**
Saturated fat **2g**
Sodium **70mg**

---

offering substitutes when these are unavailable. (The substitute is not calculated in the nutrient analysis, however.) Most of the ingredients can be found in any well-stocked supermarket; the exceptions can be bought in speciality or ethnic shops.

In Healthy Home Cooking's test kitchens, heavy-bottomed pots and pans are used to guard against foods burning and sticking when little oil is used; non-stick pans are also utilized. Both safflower oil and virgin olive oil are favoured for sautéing. Safflower was chosen because it is the most highly polyunsaturated vegetable fat available in supermarkets, and polyunsaturated fats reduce blood cholesterol; if unobtainable, use sunflower oil, also high in polyunsaturated fats. Virgin olive oil is used because it has a fine fruity flavour lacking in the lesser grade

known as "pure". In addition, it is — like all olive oil — high in monounsaturated fats, which are thought not to increase blood cholesterol. Virgin and safflower oils can be combined, with olive oil contributing its fruitiness to the safflower oil. When virgin olive oil is unavailable, "pure" may be substituted.

About cooking times

To help the cook plan ahead effectively, Healthy Home Cooking takes time into account in all of its recipes. While recognizing that everyone cooks at a different speed, and that stoves and ovens differ in temperatures, the series provides approximate "working" and "total" times for every dish. Working time stands for the minutes actively spent on preparation; total time includes unattended cooking time, as well as time devoted to marinating, chilling or soaking. Since the recipes emphasize fresh foods, they may take a bit longer to prepare than quick and easy dishes that call for canned or packaged products, but the payoff in flavour and often in nutrition should compensate for the little extra time involved.

Recommended Dietary Guidelines

		Average Daily Intake		Maximum Daily Intake			
		CALORIES	PROTEIN grams	CHOLESTEROL milligrams	TOTAL FAT grams	SATURATED FAT grams	SODIUM milligrams
Females	7-8	1900	47	300	80	32	2000*
	9-11	2050	51	300	77	35	2000
	12-17	2150	53	300	81	36	2000
	18-53	2150	54	300	81	36	2000
	54-74	1900	47	300	72	32	2000
Males	7-8	1980	49	300	80	33	2000
	9-11	2280	57	300	77	38	2000
	12-14	2640	66	300	99	44	2000
	15-17	2880	72	300	108	48	2000
	18-34	2900	72	300	109	48	2000
	35-64	2750	69	300	104	35	2000
	65-74	2400	60	300	91	40	2000

*(or 5g salt)

Hand-held delicacies

At any party where it is intended that guests should move around and mingle, perilous balancing acts with glasses, plates and cutlery are best avoided. The ideal refreshments are those that can be eaten by hand. Titbits such as small sandwiches or bread pinwheels, stuffed cherry tomatoes or mushroom caps, cheese balls rolled in herbs and spices, fresh dates filled with smoked beef and mozzarella cheese, are all easy to eat neatly with the fingers, as are morsels of seafood, such as butterfly prawns. Fresh vegetables make excellent scoops for dips, or bases for other ingredients: a crisp array of cauliflower sticks, sweet pepper strips and other crudités accompany a hot tomato dip; chicory leaves and mange-tout pods hold colourful purées of peas and carrots. Other unusual containers include anise-flavoured crêpes, formed into fans for easy dipping, or pancakes moulded and baked into crisp cups to receive a filling of broad beans in a creamy mustard sauce.

Some foods, by their very shape and structure, lend themselves naturally to being eaten with the fingers. Chicken wings or glazed drumsticks, for instance, or mussels topped with tomato and fennel and served on the half shell, are easy to handle. With the help of small skewers or cocktail sticks, other items can be conveniently speared on their own or assembled as brochettes: multicoloured, mushroom-filled tortellini, miniature kebabs of pork and fennel or turkey and cranberries, cubes of monkfish wrapped in bacon, baby baked potatoes in a coating of Parmesan cheese, are only a few of countless possibilities.

Showpieces for grand occasions

Many of the recipes in this book can be prepared in minutes. But speedy preparation is not always a priority. For an enthusiastic cook, the time spent in the kitchen before a large party or special celebration is part and parcel of the pleasure the event provides. These are the occasions when culinary artistry can flower, indeed run rampant. Yet it is possible to create a veritable feast without sending the guests' salt or saturated fat consumption soaring. Jewel-like canapés of asparagus, prawn and haddock, of carefully trimmed chicken breast or duck, all shimmering in coats of aspic, are rich only in flavour. Shells of choux pastry — made lighter by using fewer eggs than most recipes demand — can be studded with pine-nuts for an intriguing variation in texture and combined with a delicately-flavoured mushroom filling, while croustade cases are crisped in the oven with only the slightest brushing of oil, to hold scallops in a tarragon-lemon sauce, or a vibrant mixture of crabmeat, tomato and aubergine. Some presentations, such as a magnificent, multi-layered chicken and asparagus sandwich gateau, demand a fair amount of care, but amply repay these efforts by the admiration they elicit at serving time. If you are tempted to try a new and relatively complicated recipe for a special event, allow yourself, if possible, the luxury of a trial run, and let friends or family reap the benefits of this culinary dress rehearsal.

A matter of logistics

Even the most elaborate creations are simplified by a little forward planning. Yeast dough for pizzas and calzones, pastry for quiches and tartlets, fresh pasta dough and pancake batters can all be made ahead of time and stored in the refrigerator until needed; many sauces, dips and marinades will even improve in flavour if they are prepared a day or so in advance. When you are organizing a large party, save eleventh-hour panics in the kitchen by devising a menu that includes only one or two items needing last-minute attention.

If you are catering for large numbers, it is best to avoid the temptation of offering too vast an array of different dishes, confusing the eye and palate, and detracting from the appreciation each delicacy deserves. Limit the number of elements, and make whatever you choose in multiple batches: doubling or trebling the quantities in a recipe does not necessarily double or treble the time required to produce it. For ease of serving, aim for a mixture of hot and cold items, including some that will not suffer if they are set out well before your guests arrive, or that can be held in a low oven without detriment.

And, just as you would for an ordinary dinner party, compose a menu that is well-balanced in flavours, textures and appearance: a spread with too many items of the same colour, or which is accompanied by similar sauces, may be overwhelming and disappointing at the same time. The happiest results will be achieved by an imaginative mix of dishes, featuring different main ingredients, that complement each other rather than compete for attention. And, since most people now number at least one vegetarian among their acquaintances, make sure that all your guests enjoy the party by including a selection of snacks made without meat or fish.

No such advance planning is necessary, or possible, for spur-of-the-moment treats for family members or unexpected guests. Instead, take the pressure off the cook by enlisting the rest of the company as helpers to slice bread, make toast, chop herbs or assemble garnishes. With a few additional willing hands in the kitchen, even the most elaborate snack can be put together in a matter of minutes, producing results that are far more delicious, far healthier and infinitely more interesting than anything available in the over-salted, fat-laden world of so-called fast food.

Bread and Biscuits for Snacks

Bread is an integral part of many snacks, from substantial stuffed loaves to dainty sandwiches and, most delicate of all, the bite-sized canapé. The character of such snacks depends not only on the texture and flavour of the bread but on the way it is sliced, shaped, filled or garnished.

The most versatile bread is the firm, close-grained, rectangular white tin loaf *(recipe, right)*. It can be sliced to any thickness; it toasts well; and when slices are rolled out they can be used for pinwheel sandwiches or shaped into croustades. The wholemeal tin loaf *(recipe, far right)* has a more crumbly texture, making it unsuitable for moulding or for canapés but ideal for sandwiches.

The distinctive nutty flavour of the dark rye breads and pumpernickel makes them good choices for strongly flavoured foods such as smoked meats and fish. Their firm, even texture, which does not easily absorb moisture from fillings, also makes them good foundations for canapés and open sandwiches.

French loaves, or baguettes, can be split lengthwise and filled, or cut into rounds and spread with topping. The dry Middle Eastern pittas can be halved and stuffed with anything from stir-fried vegetables and meats to salads and fruits. Toasted bread or dry biscuits can accompany dips and patés.

Slightly stale bread — about a day old — is easier to slice and shape than a fresh crumbly loaf. For best results, slice it with a sharp, long-bladed cook's knife. Or ask your baker to slice the bread by machine, to ensure even slices of the required thickness.

Leftovers can be processed into crumbs and frozen, or dried in a cool airy place for two or three days, then stored in an airtight container for up to three weeks. Larger pieces may be cut into croûtons and frozen.

White Tin Loaf

Makes 1 large loaf
Working time: about 30 minutes
Total time: about 3 hours (includes rising)

15 g	fresh yeast, or 7 g (¼ oz) dried yeast	½ oz
750 g	strong plain white flour	1½ lb
2 tsp	salt	2 tsp
30 g	polyunsaturated margarine	1 oz

Calories **2,850**
Protein **75g**
Cholesterol **0mg**
Total fat **33g**
Saturated fat **7g**
Sodium **2,600mg**

Add the fresh yeast to 45 cl (¾ pint) of tepid water, stir with a fork until the yeast has completely dissolved then set aside for 10 minutes to activate; reconstitute dried yeast according to the manufacturer's instructions. Meanwhile, sift the flour and salt into a large mixing bowl, and rub in the margarine.

Make a well in the centre of the flour. Pour the yeast liquid into the well, then mix together by hand to form a firm, yet slightly sticky dough. Turn the dough on to a lightly floured surface and knead well for 10 to 15 minutes, until the dough becomes very smooth and elastic. (Avoid adding too much flour as you knead: this will make the dough dry. As the dough is kneaded it will become firmer and less sticky.) Alternatively, the dough may be mixed with a dough hook, or in a food processor with a special blade for mixing dough. (Check the manufacturer's instructions for the weight of dough your machine can mix at one time.)

Shape the kneaded dough into a neat round and place it in a clean, lightly floured, mixing bowl. Cover with plastic film and place in a warm, not hot, place for 45 minutes to 1 hour, until the dough has risen to double its original size. It should spring back when pressed with a floured finger.

Turn the risen dough on to a very lightly floured work surface and knock it back to its original size by firmly pounding it with clenched fists, to expel the air bubbles. Re-knead for 2 to 3 minutes, until smooth.

Grease a 24 by 14 by 7.5 cm (9½ by 5½ by 3 inch) loaf tin. Shape the dough into an oblong large enough to fit into the bottom of the tin. Place the dough in the tin, pressing it firmly into the corners, and loosely cover the tin with plastic film. Stand the tin in a warm, not hot, place for 30 to 45 minutes, until the dough rises to the top of the loaf tin.

Meanwhile, preheat the oven to 230°C (450°F or Mark 8). Remove the plastic film from the risen loaf, then bake the loaf for 35 to 40 minutes until it is golden-brown and has shrunk away from the sides of the tin. When it is turned out, the loaf base should sound hollow when lightly tapped with the knuckles. Place on a wire rack to cool.

Wholemeal Tin Loaf

Makes 1 large loaf
Working time: about 30 minutes
Total time: about 3 hours (includes rising)

30 g	fresh yeast, or 15 g (½ oz) dried yeast	1 oz
750 g	wholemeal flour	1½ lb
1 tbsp	dark brown sugar	1 tbsp
2 tsp	salt	2 tsp
60 g	polyunsaturated margarine	2 oz

Calories **2,900**
Protein **103g**
Cholesterol **0mg**
Total fat **64g**
Saturated fat **14g**
Sodium **2,840mg**

Make and bake the bread as directed for the white loaf above, adding the brown sugar to the sifted flour and salt.

Wholemeal Pittas

Makes 16 pittas
Working time: about 40 minutes
Total time: about 2 hours and 15 minutes
(includes rising)

30 g	fresh yeast, or 15 g (½ oz) dried yeast	1 oz
500 g	wholemeal flour	1 lb
250 g	strong plain white flour	8 oz
2 tsp	salt	2 tsp
2 tbsp	virgin olive oil	2 tbsp

Calories **170**
Protein **6g**
Cholesterol **0mg**
Total fat **3g**
Saturated fat **trace**
Sodium **150mg**

Make and rise the dough as for the white tin loaf on the left, adding the olive oil at the same time as the yeast liquid.

Knock back the risen dough, then knead until smooth. Divide the dough into 16 pieces and shape each one into a neat round. Cover the rounds with plastic film.

Taking one round at a time, roll out to an oval shape about 17.5 cm (7 inches) long, then place on a floured cloth. Cover the shaped pittas with a clean cloth and leave in a warm place for about 20 minutes to rise slightly. Meanwhile, preheat the oven to its highest setting.

Lightly oil several baking sheets and heat them in the oven for 10 minutes. Immediately, place the pittas on the hot baking sheets and bake them for about 10 minutes, until they have puffed up. Remove them to wire racks to cool.

Water Biscuits

Makes about 36 biscuits
Working time: about 20 minutes
Total time: about 35 minutes

250 g	plain flour	8 oz
½ tsp	salt	½ tsp
1 ½ tsp	baking powder	1 ½ tsp
60 g	polyunsaturated margarine	2 oz

Calories **35**
Protein **1g**
Cholesterol **0mg**
Total fat **2g**
Saturated fat **trace**
Sodium **50mg**

Preheat the oven to 190°C (375°F or Mark 5). Grease several baking sheets. Sift the flour, salt and baking powder into a large bowl. Rub the margarine into the flour until the mixture resembles fine breadcrumbs, then make a well in the centre. Add 5 to 6 tablespoons of water and mix, with a round-bladed knife, to make a firm dough.

Knead the dough on a lightly floured surface until smooth, then roll out until almost paper-thin. Prick the dough all over with a fork. Using a 7.5 cm (3 inch) plain round cutter, cut out rounds from the dough and place them on the baking sheets. Re-knead and roll out the trimmings, then cut more rounds, continuing until the dough is used up.

Bake the biscuits for 10 to 15 minutes until they are only just lightly browned. Remove to wire racks to cool.

EDITOR'S NOTE: *For herb-flavoured biscuits, add 2 teaspoons of mixed dried herbs to the sifted flour. Sesame seeds, or poppy seeds may be sprinkled over the rolled-out dough and lightly rolled into the dough before the biscuits are cut out. The water biscuits may be stored for up to one week in an airtight container.*

Melba Toast

Makes about 40 pieces
Working time: about 10 minutes
Total time: about 1 hour

½	large white tin loaf, or one small loaf, three to four days old	½

Calories **35**
Protein **1g**
Cholesterol **0mg**
Total fat **2g**
Saturated fat **trace**
Sodium **50mg**

Preheat the oven to 170°C (325°F or Mark 3). Cut away the crusts, then slice the loaf as thinly as possible. Cut each slice in two diagonally, to make two triangles. Place the triangles on baking sheets, in single layers. Bake for 50 minutes, until the bread curls nicely and turns to a crisp, pale golden-brown, toast. Spread in a single layer on a wire rack to cool. Serve cold, or re-warm in a 180°C (350°F or Mark 4) oven for 5 to 10 minutes.

EDITOR'S NOTE: *The Melba toast can be stored in an airtight container for up to two weeks.*

Chive and Oatmeal Biscuits

Makes: about 40 biscuits
Working time: about 20 minutes
Total time: about 45 minutes

125 g	rolled oats, finely ground	4 oz
125 g	plain flour	4 oz
1 tsp	baking powder	1 tsp
¼ tsp	salt	¼ tsp
1 tbsp	finely chopped fresh chives	1 tbsp
90 g	polyunsaturated margarine	3 oz

Calories **40**
Protein **1g**
Cholesterol **0mg**
Total fat **2g**
Saturated fat **trace**
Sodium **40mg**

Preheat the oven to 180°C (350°F or Mark 4). Grease several baking sheets.

Put the oats, flour, baking powder, salt and chives into a bowl and mix well together. Rub in the margarine until the mixture resembles fine breadcrumbs, then make a well in the centre. Add 3 tablespoons of boiling water and mix, with a round-bladed knife, to make a firm dough.

Knead the dough lightly on a floured surface until smooth, then roll out to about 3 mm (⅛ inch) thick. Using a 5 cm (2 inch) plain round cutter, cut out rounds from the dough and place them on the prepared baking sheets. Re-knead and roll out the pastry trimmings, then cut out more rounds, continuing until the dough is used up.

Bake the biscuits for 20 to 25 minutes, until well cooked through and very lightly browned. Remove to wire racks to cool.

EDITOR'S NOTE: *The biscuits may be stored for up to one week in an airtight container.*

1 *Vegetable strips and shreds of lemon rind lie on a bed of Japanese rice and dried seaweed ready to be rolled and sliced into eye-catching sushi (recipe, page 26).*

Cold Party Treats

Set out to greet the guests on their arrival, cold snacks are perhaps the party-giver's staunchest allies. Whether a plate of simple pretzels *(page 15)*, or a collation of exotic sushi *(left)*, they can all be prepared in advance and arranged to make an attractive display.

Alongside some intriguing newcomers, such as labne cocktail balls *(page 24)* — savoury mouthfuls moulded from strained yogurt — the recipes in this chapter include many familiar offerings, but here contrived with a lighter, healthier touch. Stuffed eggs *(page 22)*, for example, are filled with a low-fat mixture of chive-flecked ricotta cheese in place of the more usual dollops of mayonnaise. Cheese straws — normally made from high-fat puff pastry — are produced from a more wholesome dough that is low in fat and enriched with oatmeal *(page 16)*. And the chick-pea dip on page 20, inspired by the Middle Eastern snack hummus, derives its creamy texture from low-fat yogurt rather than the traditional olive oil.

Many of the dishes in this chapter can be made well ahead of time, thus easing your final workload. The various savoury appetizers, for instance, can be baked up to three days beforehand and, once cool, stored in airtight containers. Dips and sauces can be prepared a day or two ahead and kept covered with plastic film in the refrigerator until required. Other offerings should be made on the day of the party. Those containing vegetables, such as crudité skewers on page 19, should be assembled as late in the day as possible to ensure that they retain their fresh appearance and flavour. And the caviare canapés on page 25 must be put together at the last minute lest their bread bases, unprotected with butter or margarine, become soggy.

The most time-consuming but eye-catching party dishes are the aspic-coated canapés on pages 50 to 53, and for these careful planning is required. The vegetable aspic that gives them their gleaming coat can be made a couple of days before it is needed, and the main ingredients such as duck or chicken breast, can be trimmed and prepared a day before the party, wrapped in plastic film and refrigerated. The final assembly should be completed about 20 minutes before serving: late enough to ensure the decorative garnishes look fresh and bright, but early enough to allow the aspic to set in the refrigerator.

Cocktail Croûtons

Makes about 200 croûtons
Working time: about 30 minutes
Total time: about 45 minutes

Per 5 croûtons:
Calories **40**
Protein **1g**
Cholesterol **4mg**
Total fat **2g**
Saturated fat **1g**
Sodium **4mg**

12	thin slices day-old wholemeal bread, about 12 by 10 cm (5 by 4 inches) each	12
60 g	unsalted butter	2 oz
1 tbsp	Dijon mustard	1 tbsp
2	garlic cloves, crushed	2
2 tbsp	finely chopped parsley	2 tbsp
¼ tsp	salt	¼ tsp
⅛ tsp	cayenne pepper	⅛ tsp
30 g	Parmesan cheese, finely grated	1 oz

Preheat the oven to 220°C (425°F or Mark 7). Grease several baking sheets.

Remove the crusts from the bread. Put the butter into a bowl with the mustard, crushed garlic, chopped parsley, salt and cayenne pepper. Beat together until the mixture is very soft and creamy.

Spread both sides of each slice of bread very thinly with the savoury butter. Sprinkle one side of each slice of bread with the grated Parmesan, then cut each slice into about 18 small triangles, as shown here, or into squares or oblongs.

Put the bread shapes on the baking sheets and cook in the oven until they are crisp and golden-brown — 10 to 15 minutes. Serve warm or cold.

Miniature Savoury Choux Puffs

Makes about 350 puffs
Working time: about 40 minutes
Total time: about 1 hour

Per 5 puffs:
Calories **65**
Protein **1g**
Cholesterol **25mg**
Total fat **4g**
Saturated fat **2g**
Sodium **65mg**

125 g	plain flour	4 oz
¼ tsp	salt	¼ tsp
2	eggs	2
1	egg white	1
90g	polyunsaturated margarine	3 oz
60 g	Parmesan cheese, finely grated	2 oz
1	garlic clove, crushed	1
2 tbsp	finely cut fresh chives	2 tbsp
1 tbsp	mixed dried herbs	1 tbsp

Preheat the oven to 220°C (425°F or Mark 7). Line several baking sheets with non-stick baking parchment. Have ready three piping bags, each fitted with a 1 cm (½ inch) plain nozzle. Sift the flour and salt on to a small sheet of greaseproof paper. Lightly beat the eggs and the egg white together.

Put the margarine into a saucepan with ¼ litre (8 fl oz) of cold water and heat gently until the margarine melts, then bring to the boil. Remove the pan from the heat and tip in the flour, stirring quickly with a wooden spoon at the same time. Return the pan to a moderate heat and stir for a few seconds until the mixture forms a ball. Remove from the heat.

Very gradually add the eggs to the flour and water paste, beating vigorously between each addition with a wooden spoon or a hand-held electric mixer.

Beat the Parmesan and garlic into the choux paste. Put one third of the mixture into a piping bag. Put another third of the mixture into a small bowl and beat in the chives, then spoon into another piping bag. Beat the mixed herbs into the remaining choux paste and spoon into the third piping bag.

Pipe the choux mixtures on to the lined baking sheets in small mounds about 1 cm (½ inch) in diameter, spaced apart. Bake in the oven until well risen, golden-brown and crisp — 20 to 25 minutes. Remove the puffs from the baking sheets immediately and transfer to wire racks to cool. Serve the puffs within a couple of hours.

EDITOR'S NOTE: The piped dough may be stored for up to 2 hours in the refrigerator before baking. Alternatively, pipe the choux on to foil-lined trays and freeze. Then lift off each foil, stack, wrap and store in the freezer. When required, place each foil sheet on a baking sheet and bake.

Herb Pretzels

Makes about 40 pretzels
Working time: about 45 minutes
Total time: about 1 hour

Preheat the oven to 200°C (400°F or Mark 6). Grease several baking sheets.

Sift the flours, salt and baking powder into a mixing bowl, adding any bran left in the sieve. Mix in the herbs, then rub in the margarine until the mixture resembles fine breadcrumbs. Make a well in the centre of the flour. Pour 5 tablespoons of boiling water into the well, then mix with a round-bladed knife to form a soft dough. Knead the dough on a very lightly floured surface to smooth.

Divide the dough into about 40 small pieces. Take one piece of dough and roll it out with your hands into a thin strand, about 30 cm (12 inches) long.

Form a pretzel by shaping the strand into a curve, with its ends towards you. Cross the ends over, then take their points up to the centre of the curve and press them firmly in position. Place the pretzel on a baking sheet. Shape the remaining pieces of dough in the same way.

Brush the pretzels lightly with the beaten egg, then sprinkle with the Parmesan. Bake in the oven for about 15 minutes, until lightly browned. Carefully remove the pretzels to a wire rack to cool.

EDITOR'S NOTE: The pretzels may be stored in an airtight tin for up to two days.

Per 5 pretzels:			
Calories **185**	125 g	plain flour	4 oz
Protein **5g**	60 g	wholemeal flour	2 oz
Cholesterol **35mg**	¼ tsp	salt	¼ tsp
Total fat **11g**	½ tsp	baking powder	½ tsp
Saturated fat **3g**	1 tsp	mixed dried herbs	1 tsp
Sodium **205mg**	90 g	polyunsaturated margarine	3 oz
	1	small egg, beaten	1
	30 g	Parmesan cheese, finely grated	1 oz

Savoury Nibbles

Makes about 250
Working time: about 30 minutes
Total time: about 40 minutes

Per 5 nibbles:
Calories **85**
Protein **2g**
Cholesterol **20mg**
Total fat **6g**
Saturated fat **2g**
Sodium **120mg**

175 g	plain flour	6 oz
½ tsp	salt	½ tsp
½ tsp	baking powder	½ tsp
90 g	polyunsaturated margarine	3 oz
90 g	Cheddar cheese, finely grated	3 oz
1	egg, lightly beaten	1
1 tsp	curry powder	1 tsp
1	garlic clove	1
2 tbsp	finely chopped parsley	2 tbsp

Preheat the oven to 200°C (400°F or Mark 6). Grease several baking sheets.

Sift the flour, half of the salt and the baking powder into a mixing bowl. Rub the margarine into the flour until the mixture resembles fine breadcrumbs. Mix in the cheese. Add the egg and mix together with a round-bladed knife to form a soft dough.

Gently knead the dough on a lightly floured surface until smooth, then roll out to an oblong approximately 45 by 30 cm (18 by 12 inches). Using a fluted pastry wheel, cut the dough into long, thin strips, about 2 cm (¾ inch) wide. Cut across the strips to make diamond shapes, oblongs or squares. Place the tiny biscuits on the baking sheets and bake in the oven until they are golden-brown — 8 to 10 minutes. Remove the biscuits to wire racks to cool. Immediately, sift the curry powder over half of the biscuits.

Put the garlic into a small mortar with the remaining salt and crush with a pestle until creamy. Mix in the parsley. When the plain biscuits are cool, put them into a large bowl, add the garlic mixture and mix very gently until the biscuits are evenly coated. Serve the biscuits in separate bowls.

Oatmeal Cheese Straws

Makes about 100 straws
Working (and total) time: about 1 hour

Per 5 straws:
Calories **65**
Protein **2g**
Cholesterol **20mg**
Total fat **5g**
Saturated fat **2g**
Sodium **90mg**

60 g	rolled oats	2 oz
60 g	plain flour	2 oz
½ tsp	baking powder	½ tsp
¼ tsp	salt	¼ tsp
½ tsp	dry mustard	½ tsp
¼ tsp	cayenne pepper	¼ tsp
60 g	polyunsaturated margarine	2 oz
60 g	Cheddar cheese, finely grated	2 oz
30 g	Parmesan cheese, finely grated	1 oz
1	egg, beaten	1
	skimmed milk	

Preheat the oven to 200°C (400°F or Mark 6). Grease several baking sheets.

Finely grind the rolled oats in a food processor, blender or electric grinder. Sift the flour, baking powder, salt, mustard and cayenne pepper into a mixing bowl. Mix in the oats, then rub in the margarine until the mixture resembles fine breadcrumbs. Mix in the Cheddar cheese and half of the Parmesan cheese; add the egg and mix to form a soft dough. Knead the dough lightly on a floured surface to smooth.

Roll the dough out to an oblong about 30 by 22 cm (12 by 9 inches). Trim the edges to neaten, reserving the trimmings. Brush the dough with a little milk and sprinkle with the remaining Parmesan cheese. Cut the dough into three equal strips lengthwise, then cut across each strip to make 5 mm (¼ inch) wide straws. Place the cheese straws on the baking sheets, spaced slightly apart. Bake in the oven until golden-brown —

10 to 15 minutes. Very carefully remove the straws to wire racks to cool.

Meanwhile, re-knead and roll out the reserved trimmings. Using a 5 cm (2 inch) plain round cutter, cut out rounds from the dough; then, using a 3 cm (1¼ inch) plain round cutter, cut out the centre from each round to make a ring. Place the rings on a baking sheet. Re-knead and roll out the trimmings. Cut out more rings in the same way, continuing until the pastry is used up. Bake the rings for 6 to 8 minutes, until golden-brown. Carefully remove the rings to wire racks to cool.

To serve, fill each ring with straws and arrange them on a serving platter; any remaining straws may be served separately.

Sesame Crackers

Makes about 100 crackers
Working time: about 30 minutes
Total time: about 55 minutes

Per 5 crackers:
Calories **95**
Protein **3g**
Cholesterol **20mg**
Total fat **5g**
Saturated fat **3g**
Sodium **70mg**

250 g	plain flour	8 oz
¼ tsp	salt	¼ tsp
¾ tsp	baking powder	¾ tsp
60 g	unsalted butter	2 oz
90 g	Cheddar cheese, finely grated	3 oz
1	small egg, beaten	1
30 g	sesame seeds	1 oz

Preheat the oven to 200°C (400°F or Mark 6). Grease several baking sheets.

Sift the flour, salt and baking powder into a mixing bowl. Rub the butter into the flour until the mixture resembles fine breadcrumbs. Mix in the cheese, then make a well in the centre of the flour. Pour 5 tablespoons of water into the well and mix with a round-bladed knife to make a soft dough. Knead the dough on a lightly floured surface to smooth.

Roll the dough out very thinly, then prick well all over with a fork. Using a 3 cm (1¼ inch) plain round cutter, cut out rounds and place them on the baking sheets. Re-knead and re-roll the trimmings, then cut out more rounds. Continue until the dough is used up.

Brush the crackers with the beaten egg, then sprinkle with the sesame seeds. Bake in the oven until golden-brown and crisp — 20 to 25 minutes. Place the crackers on wire racks to cool.

Chili and Lime Avocado Dip

Serves 12
Working time: about 15 minutes
Total time: about 3 hours and 15 minutes
(includes setting aside)

Calories **105**
Protein **2g**
Cholesterol **0mg**
Total fat **11g**
Saturated fat **1g**
Sodium **35mg**

4	ripe avocados	4
1 tbsp	fresh lime juice	1 tbsp
1 tbsp	virgin olive oil	1 tbsp
1	pickled hot green chili pepper, finely diced (caution, right)	1
1	garlic clove, crushed	1
1	spring onion, finely chopped	1
1 tbsp	finely chopped fresh coriander	1 tbsp
¼ tsp	salt	¼ tsp
	freshly ground black pepper	

Cut the avocados in half and remove the stones. Spoon the flesh into a bowl and mash lightly with a fork — the texture should not be too smooth. Stir in the lime juice and oil, then the chili, garlic, spring onion, coriander, salt and some pepper.

Cover the mixture and set aside for at least 3 hours in order to allow the chili to permeate the dip. Serve at room temperature.

SUGGESTED ACCOMPANIMENT: *bread sticks.*

Chili Peppers—a Cautionary Note

Both dried and fresh hot chili peppers should be handled with care. Their flesh and seeds contain volatile oils that can make skin tingle and cause eyes to burn. Rubber gloves offer protection — but the cook should still be careful not to touch the face, lips or eyes when working with chilies.

Soaking fresh chilies in cold, salted water for an hour will remove some of their fire. If canned chilies are substituted for fresh ones, they should be rinsed in cold water in order to eliminate as much of the brine used to preserve them as possible.

Spiced Peanut Dip with Crudité Skewers

Serves 10
Working time: about 1 hour and 30 minutes
Total time: about 5 hours (includes chilling)

Calories **105**
Protein **5g**
Cholesterol **2mg**
Total fat **6g**
Saturated fat **1g**
Sodium **165mg**

15 cl	unsalted chicken stock (recipe, page 139)	¼ pint
1 tsp	saffron threads	1 tsp
125 g	shelled peanuts	4 oz
1 tbsp	virgin olive oil	1 tbsp
1	large onion, very finely chopped	1
4	garlic cloves, crushed	4
30 g	fresh ginger root, peeled and sliced	1 oz
2 tsp	ground coriander	2 tsp
1 tsp	ground cumin	1 tsp
1 tsp	ground cardamom	1 tsp
30 cl	plain low-fat yogurt	½ pint
½ tsp	salt	½ tsp
	freshly ground black pepper	
2 tsp	finely cut fresh chives	2 tsp
1 tsp	finely chopped parsley	1 tsp

Crudité skewers		
175 g	daikon radish, peeled	6 oz
175 g	radishes, preferably very tiny, trimmed	6 oz
175 g	carrots, peeled	6 oz
175 g	sticks celery, scrubbed	6 oz
1	small sweet red pepper, seeded and deribbed	1
1	small sweet green pepper, seeded and deribbed	1
1	small sweet yellow pepper, seeded and deribbed	1
1	small sweet orange pepper, seeded and deribbed (optional)	1

Preheat the oven to 220°C (425°F or Mark 7). In a saucepan, heat the chicken stock to boiling point; remove from the heat and add the saffron threads. Stir well and leave to stand for about 30 minutes.

Spread the peanuts out on a small baking sheet, then roast them in the oven for 6 to 8 minutes, until their skins loosen. Rub the nuts in a clean tea towel to remove their skins. Heat the oil in a saucepan; add the onions and cook gently until they are very soft but not browned — 8 to 10 minutes. Stir in the garlic.

Put the ginger, coriander, cumin, cardamom, yogurt, peanuts and saffron mixture into a blender or food processor, and blend until smooth. Pour on to the onions and stir well. Cook over low heat until the mixture thickens — about 20 minutes. Season with the salt and some pepper. Pour into a bowl; cover closely with plastic film to prevent a skin forming. When cool, chill in the refrigerator for 3 to 4 hours, or overnight.

Just before serving, prepare the vegetables. Cut them into decoratively shaped slices, as illustrated here, or into small neat cubes, and thread them on to cocktail sticks. Stir the dip and spoon it into a serving bowl, then sprinkle the top with the chives and parsley. Place the bowl on a large serving platter and surround with the crudité skewers.

EDITOR'S NOTE: *If preferred, the vegetables may be cut into 10 cm (4 inch) long sticks, and arranged round the dip.*

Chick-Pea and Yogurt Dip

THIS RECIPE IS REMINISCENT OF THE MIDDLE-EASTERN DISH
KNOWN AS HUMMUS.

Serves 6
Working time: about 15 minutes
Total time: about 2 hours (includes soaking)

Calories **145**
Protein **9g**
Cholesterol **2mg**
Total fat **3g**
Saturated fat **trace**
Sodium **160mg**

250 g	dried chick-peas	8 oz
2 tbsp	tahini	2 tbsp
12.5 cl	plain low-fat yogurt	4 fl oz
3	garlic cloves, crushed	3
2	lemons, juice only	2
½ tsp	salt	½ tsp
	freshly ground black pepper	
	paprika, for garnish	
	chopped parsley, for garnish	

Rinse the chick-peas under cold running water. Put them in a large, heavy-bottomed saucepan and pour in enough cold water to cover them by about 5 cm (2 inches). Discard any chick-peas that float to the surface. Cover the saucepan, leaving the lid ajar, and bring the water to the boil; cook for 2 minutes. Turn off the heat, cover the pan, and soak the chick-peas for at least 1 hour. Alternatively, soak the chick-peas overnight in cold water.

When the chick-peas have finished soaking, drain them well in a colander. Return them to the pan and pour in enough water to cover them by about 5 cm (2 inches). Bring the liquid to a simmer; cook the chick-peas over medium-low heat until they are quite tender — 45 minutes to 1 hour. (If they appear to be drying out at any point, pour in more water.) When cooked, drain the peas and allow them to cool.

Place the chick-peas in a food processor with the tahini, yogurt, garlic, lemon juice, salt and some freshly ground pepper. Process for about 45 seconds to produce a soft, creamy paste. Turn the dip into a shallow bowl and sprinkle with some paprika and chopped parsley before serving.

SUGGESTED ACCOMPANIMENT: *warmed pitta bread fingers.*

Garlicky Smoked Roe Dip

Serves 6
Working time: about 15 minutes
Total time: about 20 minutes

Calories **80**
Protein **6g**
Cholesterol **0mg**
Total fat **3g**
Saturated fat **trace**
Sodium **120mg**

90 g	white bread, crusts removed	3 oz
90 g	smoked cod's roe, skinned	3 oz
60 g	medium-fat curd cheese	2 oz
½	lemon, juice only	½
1	small garlic clove, crushed	1
	freshly ground black pepper	
	lemon wedges, for garnish	

Place the bread in a small bowl, cover with water and leave to soak for a few minutes.

Remove the bread from the water and squeeze it thoroughly dry, then place it in a food processor with the cod's roe, curd cheese, lemon juice, crushed garlic and some freshly ground black pepper. Process until the mixture is smooth.

Turn the purée into a small bowl and serve it garnished with the lemon wedges.

SUGGESTED ACCOMPANIMENT: *warmed pitta bread fingers.*

gently for 10 minutes. Immediately, pour off the boiling water and cool the eggs under cold running water.

Meanwhile, prepare the vegetables. Trim, wash and dry the celery sticks. Cut the sticks into 15 cm (6 inch) evenly shaped lengths. Cut half of the red pepper into fine strips; reserve 12 strips and chop the rest into small dice. Cut one third of the green pepper into dice of the same size. (The remainder of the peppers will not be needed for this recipe.)

Shell the eggs, cut each one in half lengthwise and remove the yolks. Sieve the egg yolks through a nylon sieve into a bowl, then sieve the ricotta cheese through the same sieve into the bowl. Add the *fromage frais*, salt and some pepper, and 2 tablespoons of the chives. Beat well together until smooth and creamy.

Put the egg mixture into a piping bag fitted with a medium-sized star nozzle. Pipe a whirl of mixture into each egg white, then pipe the rest into the celery.

Sprinkle the eggs with the remaining chives and garnish each one with a twisted strip of red pepper. Sprinkle half of the celery with the chopped red pepper and the other half with the green pepper. Cut the celery into 2.5 cm (1 inch) lengths. Arrange the eggs and celery on serving platters.

EDITOR'S NOTE: *The unused red and green peppers will keep well in a covered container in the refrigerator for three to four days. They can be used for salads, or in cooked dishes.*

Skinning a Sweet Pepper

LOOSENING AND REMOVING THE SKIN. Place the pepper about 5 cm (2 inches) below a preheated grill. Turn the pepper as its sides become slightly scorched, until the skin has blistered all round. Transfer the pepper to a bowl and cover with plastic film, or put the pepper in a paper bag and fold it shut; the trapped steam will make the pepper limp and loosen its skin. With a paring knife, peel off the pepper's skin in sections, from top to bottom. The pepper may then be seeded and deribbed.

Stuffed Eggs and Celery

Makes 60 pieces
Working (and total) time: about 40 minutes

Per piece:		
Calories **15**	6	eggs	6
Protein **1g**	8	sticks celery	8
Cholesterol **10mg**	1	small sweet red pepper, skinned (right), seeded and deribbed	1
Total fat **1g**			
Saturated fat **trace**	1	small sweet green pepper, skinned (right), seeded and deribbed	1
Sodium **30mg**			
	125 g	low-fat ricotta cheese	4 oz
	100 g	fromage frais	3½ oz
	¼ tsp	salt	¼ tsp
		freshly ground black pepper	
	3 tbsp	finely cut fresh chives	3 tbsp

Put the eggs into a saucepan and cover with cold water. Bring the water to the boil and cook the eggs

Anise Crêpe Fans with Herbed Dip

Makes 24 crêpe fans
Working time: about 30 minutes
Total time: about 1 hour

Per crêpe fan:			
Calories **40**	125 g	fine plain flour	4 oz
Protein **1g**	¼ tsp	salt	¼ tsp
Cholesterol **10mg**	1	egg	1
Total fat **1g**	15 cl	skimmed milk	¼ pint
Saturated fat **trace**	1 tbsp	anise-flavoured spirit	1 tbsp
Sodium **5mg**	1 tbsp	virgin olive oil	1tbsp
	2 tbsp	chopped fresh chervil	2 tbsp
	¼ tsp	ground star anise (optional)	¼ tsp
	¼ tsp	safflower oil	¼ tsp
	Herbed dip		
	175 g	thick Greek yogurt	6 oz
	½ tbsp	mild grainy mustard	½ tbsp
	1 tsp	grated lemon rind	1 tsp
	1 tsp	honey	1 tsp
	2 tbsp	chopped fresh basil, or six leaves fresh young sorrel, finely shredded	2 tbsp

Sift the flour and salt into a mixing bowl. Make a well in the centre of the flour and add the egg and milk. Pour in just under 15 cl (¼ pint) of water, then beat the egg, milk and water together with a wire whisk or wooden spoon, gradually drawing in the flour. When no lumps remain, stir in the anise-flavoured spirit, olive oil, chervil and star anise, if using. Leave to rest for about 30 minutes. The batter should be the consistency of thin cream; if it is thicker, add more water.

Heat a 25 cm (10 inch) crêpe pan or non-stick frying pan *(page 86)* over medium-high heat. Add the safflower oil and spread it over the entire surface with a paper towel. Put about 3 tablespoons of the batter into the hot pan and immediately swirl the pan to coat the bottom with a thin, even layer of batter. Pour any excess batter back into the bowl. Cook the crêpe until the bottom is browned — about 1 minute. Lift the edge with a spatula and turn the crêpe over. Cook the crêpe on the second side until it, too, is browned — 15 to 30 seconds. Slide the crêpe on to a plate. Repeat the process with the remaining batter, stirring the batter between each crêpe; if the pan looks matt and dry, wipe it again with a little oil. Stack the cooked crêpes on the plate as you go; cover them with a towel and set them aside. There should be enough batter to make six or seven crêpes.

Preheat the oven to 190°C (375°F or Mark 5). Using a sharp knife or kitchen scissors, cut each crêpe into quarters; fold each quarter in three, speckled side outwards. Place the crêpe fans on non-stick or lightly greased baking sheets and bake until crisp on the outside (a little of the centre will remain soft) — about 15 minutes. Place on a wire rack to cool.

To make the dip, stir together the yogurt, mustard, lemon rind, honey and basil or sorrel. Place in a serving bowl and keep in a cool place until ready to serve.

Labne Cocktail Balls

LABNE IS A MIDDLE EASTERN YOGURT CHEESE TRADITIONALLY
MADE FROM EWE'S MILK YOGURT.

Makes about 24 labne balls
Working time: about 20 minutes
Total time: about 26 hours (includes draining)

Per 3 balls:
Calories **70**
Protein **3g**
Cholesterol **10mg**
Total fat **3g**
Saturated fat **2g**
Sodium **35mg**

500 g	unstirred and unstrained ewe's milk yogurt	1 lb
2 tsp	coriander seeds, toasted and lightly crushed ·	2 tsp
2 tbsp	medium-grade oatmeal, toasted	2 tbsp
2 tsp	black poppy seeds, toasted	2 tsp
4 tbsp	finely chopped mixed fresh herbs such as parsley, chervil, mint, tarragon and lemon balm	4 tbsp

To make the labne, line a large sieve with a single layer of dampened muslin. Place the sieve over a deep bowl and gently spoon the yogurt into the sieve.

Cover the bowl and sieve with plastic film and set aside for about 2 hours to start the initial separation of curds and whey. Then put the sieve and bowl into the refrigerator and let the yogurt continue draining for about 24 hours to form a firm thick curd in the sieve.

When the labne is ready, add the crushed coriander seeds and mix well. Place the oatmeal on a shallow plate, the poppy seeds on another and the fresh herbs on a third. Using a melon baller, miniature ice-cream scoop or two teaspoons, make small balls of curd and drop some on to each of the three coatings. Carefully roll the balls until they are well coated, then arrange them on a serving dish and refrigerate until required.

EDITOR'S NOTE: *Labne may be made in advance and kept in the refrigerator, covered with plastic film, for two or three days. To toast coriander and poppy seeds, place them in a heavy-bottomed pan over high heat and cook until they darken slightly, bounce and release their aroma — 1 to 2 minutes; shake the pan to keep the seeds moving. Toast oatmeal in the same way until golden.*

Dates Stuffed with Bresaola and Mozzarella

Makes 30 stuffed dates
Working (and total) time: about 15 minutes

Per stuffed date:			
Calories **20**	1 tbsp	virgin olive oil	1 tbsp
Protein **1g**		freshly ground black pepper	
Cholesterol **1mg**	125 g	mozzarella, cut into 30 sticks about	4 oz
Total fat **2g**		5 by 1 by 1 cm (2 by ½ by ½ inch)	
Saturated fat **1g**	15	fresh dates, halved, stones	15
Sodium **40mg**		removed	
	30 g	bresaola, cut into 1 cm (½ inch)	1 oz
		wide ribbons	
		fresh parsley sprigs, for garnish	

Pour the olive oil into a shallow dish, grind in some black pepper and add the mozzarella; carefully turn the cheese sticks in the oil to coat them thoroughly. Arrange the date halves, cut sides up, on a serving platter. Wind the ribbons of bresaola diagonally round the sticks of mozzarella, and lay them on the date halves. Serve garnished with the sprigs of parsley.

Caviare Canapés

Makes 18 canapés
Working (and total) time: about 15 minutes

Per canapé:			
Calories **20**	3	slices dark pumpernickel	3
Protein **1g**	150 g	fromage frais	5 oz
Cholesterol **10mg**	20 g	black caviare or lumpfish roe	¾ oz
Total fat **1g**	20 g	red caviare or lumpfish roe	¾ oz
Saturated fat **trace**			
Sodium **55mg**			

Cut each slice of pumpernickel in half lengthwise, then cut each half into three to make six pieces about 4 cm (1½ inches) square. Arrange the pumpernickel squares on a serving dish or plate.

Spread a little of the *fromage frais* on to the centre of each piece of pumpernickel, leaving the edges of the bread showing. Spoon about ¼ teaspoon of black roe on to half the bread squares, then spoon a smaller amount of red roe on to the middle of the black roe. Spoon the red roe on to the remaining bread squares, with a smaller amount of black roe on top. Serve the canapés immediately.

Sesame Sushi

THE SUSHI IN THIS RECIPE IS WRAPPED IN NORI, A DARK GREEN
SEAWEED SOLD PRESSED IN SHEETS AND DRIED, WHICH IS
LIGHTLY TOASTED BEFORE USE.

Makes 16 sushi
Working time: about 40 minutes
Total time: about 1 hour and 30 minutes

Per sushi:
Calories **65**
Protein **2g**
Cholesterol **0mg**
Total fat **1g**
Saturated fat **trace**
Sodium **75mg**

200 g	sushi rice	7 oz
1 tsp	salt	1 tsp
2 tsp	sugar	2 tsp
3 tbsp	rice vinegar	3 tbsp
1 tbsp	sesame seeds	1 tbsp
1 tsp	low-sodium soy sauce or shoyu	1 tsp
⅛ tsp	wasabi powder	⅛ tsp
1 tbsp	dark tahini	1 tbsp
2	sheets nori	2

Place the rice in a large bowl, add about five times its
volume of cold water, stir gently, then carefully pour off
the water. Repeat the rinsing twice more to wash away
excess starch. Drain the rice and leave it in a sieve for
about 45 minutes to allow the grains to absorb any
residual water.

Put the rice in a saucepan with ¼ litre (8 fl oz) of
water and bring to the boil, partially covered, over high
heat. Reduce the heat to very low, cover and simmer
for 10 minutes. Leave the pan on the cooker, with the
heat turned off, for another 10 to 15 minutes. Dissolve
the salt and sugar in 2 tablespoons of the vinegar, and
mix into the cooked rice with a wet wooden spoon.

Place the sesame seeds in a heavy frying pan and
toast over moderate heat, stirring the seeds around,
until they turn golden — 2 to 3 minutes.

Mix 2 teaspoons of the vinegar, the soy sauce,
wasabi powder and tahini into a paste; add a little
more vinegar if required to give a creamy consistency.
In a small bowl, mix the remaining vinegar with 3
tablespoons of water. Toast one sheet of nori by
waving it about 12.5 cm (5 inches) above a high flame
for a few seconds, until it turns papery, then lay it out
on a bamboo rolling mat with a longer edge towards
you. Moisten your fingers in the bowl of water and
vinegar, and use them to spread half of the rice over
the nori; moisture from the rice will soften the nori.
Spread the rice evenly up to the two long sides of the
nori, and firm it down with your fingertips.

Using a palette knife or the back of a spoon, spread
half of the tahini paste over the rice. Reserve some of
the sesame seeds for a garnish, then sprinkle half of
the remaining seeds evenly on top of the paste.

With the help of the rolling mat, roll up the covered
sheet of nori *(page 28)*. Toast the second sheet of nori,

spread it with the remaining rice, tahini paste and
sesame seeds, and roll it up in the same way. Cut
each roll into eight pieces, wiping the knife with a
damp cloth after each cut. Place the slices on a serving plate and sprinkle over them the reserved sesame
seeds, following the spiral pattern.

EDITOR'S NOTE: *Italian short-grain rice may be used instead of
sushi rice. English mustard may be substituted for wasabi
powder. Sheets of nori for making sushi — labelled yaki sushi
nori — come in a standard size of 20 by 18 cm (8 by 7
inches). Bamboo rolling mats are sold in Japanese groceries;
a small rush table mat, or several layers of parchment paper,
may be used instead.*

Avocado Sushi with Olives and Peppers

Makes 24 sushi
Working time: about 50 minutes
Total time: about 1 hour and 30 minutes

150 g	sushi rice	5 oz
½ tsp	salt	½ tsp
1 ½ tsp	sugar	1 ½ tsp
1	lemon, juice strained, rind of one quarter pared	1
2	spring onions	2
½	small firm avocado	½
½	small sweet red pepper, skinned (page 22), seeded and deribbed	½
20	black olives, stoned	20
⅛ tsp	wasabi powder	⅛ tsp
1 tsp	rice vinegar	1 tsp
4	sheets nori	4

Per sushi:
Calories **40**
Protein **1g**
Cholesterol **0mg**
Total fat **2g**
Saturated fat **trace**
Sodium **35mg**

Put the rice in a large bowl and add about five times
its volume of water. Stir gently, then carefully pour off
the water. Repeat the rinsing twice, then drain the rice
and leave it in a sieve for about 45 minutes to allow
the grains to absorb any residual water.

Put the rice in a saucepan with ¼ litre (8 fl oz) of
water and bring to the boil, partially covered, over high
heat. Reduce the heat to very low, cover the pan and
simmer for 10 minutes. Leave the pan on the stove,
with the heat turned off, for 10 to 15 minutes. Dissolve
the salt and sugar in 2 tablespoons of the lemon juice,
and mix into the rice with a wet wooden spoon.

Blanch the lemon rind in boiling water for 5 seconds, refresh in cold water, then drain and dry the rind with paper towels. Cut the lemon rind and the spring onions into fine slivers. Peel the avocado and cut the flesh into 5 mm (¼ inch) wide strips. Toss the avocado strips gently with 1 teaspoon of the remaining lemon juice to prevent them from discolouring. Cut the pepper into narrow strips. Trim off both ends of the olives, then cut in half lengthwise. Mix the wasabi powder with a little water to make a paste.

In a small bowl, mix the vinegar with 3 tablespoons of water. Trim off a third of each nori sheet with kitchen scissors along a long edge, and discard. Divide the rice into four portions. Toast one piece of nori by waving it about 12.5 cm (5 inches) above a high flame for a few seconds until it turns papery, then lay it out on a bamboo rolling mat with a long edge towards you. Moisten your fingers in the bowl of vinegar and water.

Starting at the edge nearest you, spread one portion of the rice over about three quarters of a toasted nori sheet, firming the rice with your fingertips; moisture from the rice will soften the nori.

Smear a line of wasabi paste along the middle of the rice. Place a quarter of the olive halves end to end on the wasabi paste, a quarter of the avocado strips on top of the olives, then add a quarter of the pepper strips, slivers of spring onion and lemon rind. With the help of the rolling mat, roll up the covered sheet of nori *(page 28)*; the uncovered strip will wrap round the roll, adhering to itself.

Repeat with the remaining nori and filling ingredients to make three more rolls. Cut each roll into six slices, wiping the knife with a damp cloth after each cut, and arrange the slices on a serving plate.

EDITOR'S NOTE: *Italian short-grain rice may be used instead of sushi rice, dry mustard instead of wasabi powder.*

Rolling Sushi

1 *STARTING THE ROLLING. Place a slatted mat on the work surface; lay a sheet of nori seaweed at one end of the mat, parallel with the slats. Following the recipe, arrange the sushi ingredients on the nori sheet. Carefully lift up the end of the mat and turn the end over the ingredients to begin the roll.*

2 *COMPLETING THE ROLL. Roll the mat away from you, pressing firmly with your fingers and palms, to make a cylinder. Use the mat to roll the cylinder backwards and forwards several times to compact the rice.*

Prunes Stuffed with Wild Rice and Turkey

Makes 14 stuffed prunes
Working time: about 30 minutes
Total time: about 1 hour and 30 minutes

Per stuffed prune:
Calories **25**
Protein **2g**
Cholesterol **5mg**
Total fat **trace**
Saturated fat **trace**
Sodium **30mg**

30 g	wild rice	1 oz
¼ litre	unsalted chicken, beef or veal stock (recipes, page 139), or water	8 fl oz
14	large ready-to-eat prunes	14
60 g	smoked turkey or chicken, finely chopped	2 oz
	freshly grated nutmeg	
¼ tsp	salt	¼ tsp
	freshly ground black pepper	
1 tbsp	finely cut chives	1 tbsp

Put the rice and stock or water into a heavy-bottomed saucepan, bring to the boil, then simmer, covered, until the husks of the rice have split — 50 to 60 minutes. Drain off any remaining cooking liquid and set the rice aside to cool.

Using a sharp knife, slit open one side of each prune from end to end. Mix the turkey with the rice, season with some nutmeg, the salt and a little pepper, and stuff the prunes with this mixture. Sprinkle the chives over the stuffed prunes and serve.

EDITOR'S NOTE: *The prunes used in this recipe are sold for eating straight from the packet, and do not require either pre-soaking or stoning. If you use ordinary dried prunes, soak them for 10 minutes in boiling water with a dash of Madeira, and then stone them.*

Choux Puffs with Mushroom and Pine-Nut Filling

Makes 30 puffs
Working time: about 1 hour and 10 minutes
Total time: about 1 hour and 30 minutes

Per puff:			
Calories **50**	60 g	unsalted butter	2 oz
Protein **2g**	75 g	plain flour	2½ oz
Cholesterol **25mg**	¼ tsp	salt	¼ tsp
Total fat **4g**	2	eggs	2
Saturated fat **2g**		paprika, for garnish	
Sodium **40mg**	**Mushroom filling**		
	30 g	unsalted butter	1 oz
	750 g	mushrooms, roughly chopped	1½ lb
	1	small onion or four shallots, chopped	1
	1	garlic clove, crushed	1
	2 tbsp	finely chopped fresh tarragon, or 1 tbsp finely chopped fresh dill	2 tbsp
	½ tsp	grated nutmeg	½ tsp
	¼ tsp	salt	¼ tsp
		freshly ground black pepper	
	1 tbsp	dry sherry or brandy	1 tbsp
	1 tbsp	sherry vinegar	1 tbsp
	2 tbsp	fine fresh breadcrumbs	2 tbsp
	30 g	pine-nuts, lightly toasted	1 oz

First make the filling. Melt the butter in a heavy frying pan over medium heat; add the mushrooms and sauté them for 2 to 3 minutes. Add the onion or shallots, garlic, tarragon or dill, nutmeg, salt and some pepper, and continue to sauté until the mushrooms are soft — 7 to 10 minutes.

Using a slotted spoon, transfer the mushrooms to a food processor, leaving the cooking juices in the pan. Add the sherry or brandy and the sherry vinegar to the juices in the pan and reduce rapidly over high heat until only about 2 tablespoons remain.

Add the liquid to the mushrooms. Process the mushrooms until smooth, then add the breadcrumbs and pine-nuts and process again. Check the consistency of the mixture: it should be quite dry, otherwise the choux puffs will become soggy when filled. If necessary, add more breadcrumbs. Refrigerate the filling while you make the choux puffs.

Preheat the oven to 220°C (425°F or Mark 7). Line a large baking sheet with foil or non-stick parchment paper. Sift the flour and salt on to a small sheet of greaseproof paper, and lightly beat the eggs.

To make the dough, put the butter and 15 cl (¼ pint) of water in a saucepan over low heat to melt the butter without evaporating any water. Then bring the butter and water to the boil, remove the pan from the heat and add the flour and salt, stirring continuously with a wooden spoon. Return the pan to a low heat and cook until the mixture forms a ball in the centre of the pan. Remove from the heat and add the eggs a little at a time, mixing well after each addition.

Using a piping bag fitted with a 1 cm (½ inch) plain nozzle, make 30 little choux mounds about 2 cm (¾ inch) in diameter on the prepared baking sheet, spaced apart. Alternatively, use a teaspoon to make the shapes. Lightly flatten any little ripples or peaks with a wet teaspoon or finger.

Bake the choux until well risen and golden at the sides as well as on top — 20 to 25 minutes. Remove the puffs from the oven and pierce each with a small pointed knife to allow the steam to escape, then return to the oven for 4 to 5 minutes to dry out completely. Transfer the puffs to a wire rack to cool.

Fill the choux puffs as near to serving time as possible. Slice off the top third of each puff and place a teaspoon of the mushroom filling inside. Replace the tops. Using a fine-meshed sieve or tea-strainer, sprinkle a little paprika on top of each puff.

EDITOR'S NOTE: *To serve the puffs warm, fill them as described above, then heat them in a 220°C (425°F or Mark 7) oven for 5 to 6 minutes.*

Crêpe Cups with Broad Bean and Mushroom Filling

Makes about 36 cups
Working time: about 40 minutes
Total time: about 1 hour and 20 minutes

Per cup:
Calories **30**
Protein **1g**
Cholesterol **5mg**
Total fat **1g**
Saturated fat **0g**
Sodium **30mg**

125 g	plain flour	4 oz
¼ tsp	salt	¼ tsp
1	egg	1
15 cl	skimmed milk	¼ pint
15 cl	light beer	¼ pint
1 tbsp	light sesame oil	1 tbsp
½ tsp	safflower oil	½ tsp
	Bean and mushroom filling	
250 g	shelled fresh or frozen broad beans	8 oz
15 g	fresh chervil	½ oz
15 cl	plain low-fat yogurt	¼ pint
1 tbsp	wholegrain beer mustard	1 tbsp
¼ tsp	salt	¼ tsp
250 g	tiny button mushrooms, wiped clean and chopped to broad bean size	8 oz

To make the crêpe batter, sift the flour and salt into a bowl. Make a well in the centre of the flour and add the egg, milk and most of the beer. Beat the liquid ingredients together with a wire whisk or wooden spoon, gradually drawing in the flour, until no lumps remain. Stir in the sesame oil and leave the batter to rest for about 30 minutes. It should be the consistency of thin cream; if it is too thick, add the remaining beer.

Heat a large crêpe or non-stick frying pan over medium-high heat. Pour in the safflower oil and spread it over the entire surface with a paper towel. Drop 1 tablespoon of the batter on to the pan, and use the back of a spoon to spread the batter into a round of about 7.5 cm (3 inches) in diameter. Form two or three more crêpes until the pan is filled. Cook until the bottoms are browned — about 1 minute — then turn with a spatula and brown the other sides — 15 to 30 seconds. Slide the crêpes on to a plate. Repeat with the remaining batter, brushing the pan lightly with a little more oil if the crêpes begin to stick. Stack the cooked crêpes on the plate as you go, cover with a tea towel and set aside. There should be about 36 crêpes.

Preheat the oven to 190°C (375°F or Mark 5). Place the crêpes inside 9 cm (3½ inch) diameter brioche tins to form cups. (The tins do not require greasing, even if not non-stick.) Bake the crêpes until crisp — 10 to 15 minutes; check them as they cook to ensure that the edges do not burn. Then place the crêpe cups on a wire rack to cool.

While the cups are baking, prepare the filling. Bring 1 litre (1 ¾ pints) of water to the boil in a saucepan. Cook the broad beans in the water until barely tender — 8 to 10 minutes — then drain them. (If you are using frozen beans, cook them in 6 cl/2 fl oz of boiling water for 6 to 10 minutes.)

Set aside some chervil leaves for garnish, then finely chop the remaining leaves and blend them with the yogurt, mustard and salt. Slip off the skin from each bean and stir the beans into the yogurt mixture together with the mushrooms.

Fill the pancake cups with the bean and mushroom filling just before serving; the cups will go soft if filled in advance. Garnish with the reserved chervil leaves.

EDITOR'S NOTE: *Ordinary grainy mustard may be substituted for the milder wholegrain beer mustard.*

Stuffed Cherry Tomatoes

Makes about 20 stuffed tomatoes
Working (and total) time: about 30 minutes

Per stuffed tomato:	250 g	cherry tomatoes	8 oz
Calories **20**	125 g	medium-fat curd cheese	4 oz
Protein **1g**	2 tsp	chopped fresh basil	2 tsp
Cholesterol **trace**			
Total fat **2g**	⅛ tsp	salt	⅛ tsp
Saturated fat **0g**		freshly ground black pepper	
Sodium **25mg**		parsley leaves, for garnish	

Slice the bottoms off the tomatoes and, using a small vegetable baller or a teaspoon, scoop out the seeds and juice into a sieve placed over a small bowl. Press the juice from the seeds and discard the seeds. Mix the cheese with the chopped basil, salt, a little freshly ground pepper and about 3 teaspoons of the tomato juice, to make a soft paste.

Using a piping bag fitted with a 1 cm (½ inch) star nozzle, pipe a rosette of the curd cheese mixture into each tomato. Garnish each filled tomato with a tiny piece of parsley, and arrange them on a serving plate.

Mange-Tout with Two Purées

Makes about 36 mange-tout
Working time: about 30 minutes
Total time: about 45 minutes

125 g	mange-tout		4 oz
Cumin-scented carrot purée			
125 g	carrots, peeled and sliced into 5 mm (¼ inch) rounds		4 oz
¼ tsp	ground cumin		¼ tsp
1 tbsp	fromage frais		1 tbsp
2 tsp	fresh breadcrumbs		2 tsp
⅛ tsp	salt		⅛ tsp
	white pepper		
Minted pea purée			
3	shallots, finely chopped		3
1 tsp	unsalted butter		1 tsp
350 g	fresh peas, shelled, or 125 g (4 oz) frozen peas, thawed		12 oz
½ tsp	finely chopped fresh mint		½ tsp
1 tbsp	fromage frais		1 tbsp
2 tsp	fresh breadcrumbs		2 tsp
⅛ tsp	salt		⅛ tsp

Per 3 carrot mange-tout:
Calories **25**
Protein **2g**
Cholesterol **0mg**
Total fat **trace**
Saturated fat **trace**
Sodium **20mg**

Per 3 pea mange-tout:
Calories **40**
Protein **3g**
Cholesterol **2mg**
Total fat **1g**
Saturated fat **trace**
Sodium **15mg**

Place the mange-tout in a deep, heatproof bowl and pour a kettle of boiling water over them. Drain immediately in a colander and refresh under cold running water. Leave the mange-tout in the colander to drain.

To make the carrot purée, put the carrots into a saucepan with cold water to barely cover, add the cumin, bring to the boil and cook until the carrots are soft — 15 to 20 minutes. Drain over a bowl. Return the cooking liquid to the pan and reduce over high heat until only about a teaspoonful remains. Purée the carrots with the reduced cooking liquid in a blender, food processor or vegetable mill. If a smoother texture is preferred pass the purée through a fine-meshed sieve. If the purée is watery, cook it briefly in a saucepan over very low heat to dry it out a little. Stir in the *fromage frais* and breadcrumbs, season with the salt and some pepper, then set the mixture aside.

For the pea purée, sweat the shallots in the butter until transparent. Add the peas and 2 tablespoons of water. Heat gently until the water has completely evaporated, then remove from the heat, add the mint and stir well. Purée the peas in a food processor or blender, and stir in the *fromage frais*, breadcrumbs and salt. Set the mixture aside.

Arrange the mange-tout on serving dishes. Using a piping bag fitted with a fine nozzle, pipe the carrot purée in a line down the centre of half of the mange-tout. Then pipe the pea purée on to the remaining mange-tout. Serve cold.

Artichoke-Stuffed Mushrooms

Makes 20 stuffed mushrooms
Working time: about 30 minutes
Total time: about 40 minutes

Per mushroom:
Calories **20**
Protein **trace**
Cholesterol **0mg**
Total fat **2g**
Saturated fat **1g**
Sodium **35mg**

20	open cup mushrooms, wiped clean, stems removed	20
1	lemon, juice only	1
30 g	polyunsaturated margarine	1 oz
Artichoke stuffing		
4	small, or two large, artichokes trimmed down to the hearts, chokes removed	4
2 tsp	red wine vinegar	2 tsp
½ tsp	Dijon mustard	½ tsp
¼ tsp	salt	¼ tsp
	freshly ground black pepper	
1	garlic clove, crushed	1
¼ tsp	ground cardamom	¼ tsp
1 tbsp	virgin olive oil	1 tbsp
1 tbsp	chopped flat-leaf parsley, plus flat-leaf parsley sprigs for garnish	1 tbsp

Put the stemmed mushrooms into a large bowl with the lemon juice. Toss them gently together, and set aside for 5 to 10 minutes.

Cook the artichoke hearts in boiling water until tender — 5 to 6 minutes. Drain in a colander and refresh under cold running water. Drain and set aside.

Melt the margarine in a wide sauté pan or heavy frying pan with a lid. Place the mushrooms in a single layer in the pan, rounded sides down. Cover and cook until they just begin to soften — 2 to 3 minutes (do not overcook, as they will lose their shape). Using a slotted spoon, lift the mushrooms from the pan on to paper towels to drain and cool.

For the stuffing, put the vinegar, mustard, salt, some pepper, garlic, cardamom, oil and chopped parsley into a bowl and whisk together. Finely chop the artichoke hearts and add them to the bowl. Mix well.

Spoon the artichoke mixture into the mushrooms, mounding it neatly. Garnish each one with a tiny sprig of parsley, then arrange the stuffed mushrooms neatly on a serving dish.

EDITOR'S NOTE: *If preferred, the mushroom cups may be left raw after being tossed in the lemon juice.*

Citrus Haddock Seviche Sticks

SEVICHE IS A SPANISH WORD FOR RAW FISH "COOKED" IN AN ACIDIC MARINADE; ONLY THE FRESHEST FISH SHOULD BE USED.

Makes 60 sticks
Working time: about 1 hour
Total time: about 6 hours (includes marinating)

Per 3 sticks:
Calories **25**
Protein **5g**
Cholesterol **15mg**
Total fat **1g**
Saturated fat **trace**
Sodium **70mg**

500 g	haddock fillet	1 lb
½	cucumber	½
¼ tsp	salt	¼ tsp
3	large oranges	3
1 tbsp	virgin olive oil	1 tbsp
1 tsp	Dijon mustard	1 tsp
	freshly ground black pepper	
2 tbsp	chopped fresh basil, or 2 tsp dried basil	2 tbsp
Citrus marinade		
1 tbsp	virgin olive oil	1 tbsp
2 tbsp	fresh lemon juice, strained	2 tbsp
2 tbsp	fresh lime juice, strained	2 tbsp
2 tbsp	chopped parsley	2 tbsp
¼ tsp	salt	¼ tsp
	freshly ground black pepper	

Rinse the fillet under cold running water and pat it dry with paper towels. Using a very sharp knife, carefully remove the skin from the fillet, and remove any visible bones. Cut the fillet lengthwise into strips about 1 cm (½ inch) wide, then cut across the strips to make 60 squares. Remove any remaining bones.

For the marinade, put the oil, lemon and lime juices, parsley, salt and some pepper into a shallow non-reactive dish and whisk well together. Add the haddock pieces and turn gently until they are well coated. Cover the dish and put it into the refrigerator. Leave the haddock to marinate for at least 5 hours, turning the pieces over in the marinade two or three times.

About 1 hour before you are ready to assemble the seviche sticks, prepare the cucumber and oranges. Remove the skin from the cucumber, then cut it in half lengthwise and scoop out the seeds. Cut each piece of cucumber in half again lengthwise, then cut into 5 mm (¼ inch) thick slices. Put the cucumber pieces into a bowl and sprinkle them with the salt. Cover and set aside for about 30 minutes.

Using a small, sharp knife, remove the peel and all of the white pith from the oranges. Holding each orange over a small bowl to catch the juice, slice between flesh and membrane to remove the segments. Cut each segment into two or three pieces, depending on the size of the orange, to make 60 pieces in all. Put the oil, mustard, some black pepper, and 1 tablespoon of the orange juice into a bowl. Whisk well together, then stir in the basil. Add the orange segments and mix very gently until they are well coated. Cover and set aside until needed.

To assemble the seviche sticks, thoroughly drain the marinated haddock and the salted cucumber. Thread the haddock, cucumber and orange segments on to cocktail sticks. Arrange neatly in a shallow bowl, or spear into large oranges. Keep the seviche sticks refrigerated until ready to serve.

Herring Roe Canapés

Makes 24 canapés
Working (and total) time: about 25 minutes

Per canapé:
Calories **20**
Protein **1g**
Cholesterol **30mg**
Total fat **1g**
Saturated fat **0g**
Sodium **35mg**

250 g	soft herring roe	8 oz
1 tsp	grapeseed oil	1 tsp
½ tsp	Dijon mustard	½ tsp
1 tbsp	crème fraîche	1 tbsp
½ tsp	fresh lemon juice	½ tsp
2 tsp	finely cut chives, plus a few chives for garnish	2 tsp
⅛ tsp	cayenne pepper	⅛ tsp
1	small loaf dark rye bread, cut into thin slices	1
24	small capers, rinsed and drained	24

Rinse the roe and cut away any dark blood vessels with a pair of scissors. Gently wipe the roe clean.

Heat the grapeseed oil in a heavy frying pan over medium heat, and fry the roe gently with the mustard for 4 to 5 minutes; break up the roe with a spoon while it is cooking. Place the cooked roe in a fine-meshed nylon sieve, drain off any remaining liquid, then press the roe through the sieve into a bowl. Mix the *crème fraîche*, lemon juice, finely cut chives and cayenne pepper into the roe.

Using a 4 cm (1½ inch) round fluted pastry cutter, cut out 24 rounds from the rye bread. Spread the roe mixture on the bread circles, and garnish with the capers and chives. Arrange the canapés on a serving plate.

Anchovy Toasts

Makes 16 toasts
Working time: about 15 minutes
Total time: about 40 minutes

Per toast:
Calories **50**
Protein **1g**
Cholesterol **5mg**
Total fat **4g**
Saturated fat **1g**
Sodium **180mg**

4	thin slices bread	4
45 g	small anchovy fillets, rinsed and drained	1 ½ oz
60 g	polyunsaturated margarine	2 oz
½ tsp	fresh lemon juice	½ tsp
⅛ tsp	cayenne pepper	⅛ tsp
	freshly ground black pepper	
	parsley or lemon wedges, for garnish (optional)	

Preheat the oven to 180°C (350°F or Mark 4). Cut out a diamond-shaped piece of cardboard with sides 5 cm (2 inches) long, and use this template to cut 16 diamonds from the slices of bread. Place the bread diamonds on a baking sheet in the oven and bake them until golden on both sides, turning if necessary — about 25 minutes. Set aside to cool.

Reserve four whole anchovy fillets, and pound the rest in a mortar until a smooth paste is obtained. Gradually beat in the margarine and season with the lemon juice, cayenne pepper and some black pepper.

Spread the anchovy mixture evenly on to the diamond toasts, then draw the tines of a fork through the mixture to produce decorative lines. Cut each of the reserved anchovies into four long, thin strips. Twist each strip and lay it on top of a toast. Serve garnished, if you like, with parsley or lemon wedges.

Green-Jacket Dublin Bay Prawns

Makes 12 prawns
Working (and total) time: about 40 minutes

Per prawn:
Calories **30**
Protein **4g**
Cholesterol **25mg**
Total fat **0g**
Saturated fat **0g**
Sodium **200mg**

12	fresh or frozen Dublin Bay prawns (about 750 g/1 ½ lb)	12
12	spinach leaves, about 10 cm (4 inches) long	12
3 tbsp	low-sodium soy sauce or shoyu	3 tbsp
3 tbsp	mirin	3 tbsp
3 tsp	wasabi powder (optional)	3 tsp
Poaching liquid		
15 cl	dry white wine	¼ pint
1	onion or shallot, sliced	1
1	carrot, diced	1
2	sticks celery, diced	2
1	bay leaf, fresh or dry	1
5	parsley sprigs	5
2	fresh thyme, dill or wild fennel sprigs	2
1 tsp	salt	1 tsp
5	black peppercorns	5

For the poaching liquid, pour 1.5 to 2 litres (2½ to 3½ pints) of water into a large fireproof casserole and add the wine, onion, carrot, celery, bay leaf, herbs, salt and peppercorns. Bring the liquid to the boil, reduce the heat and simmer for 10 minutes. Rinse the prawns under cold running water, then put them in the liquid; cover the casserole and simmer for 5 to 8 minutes.

While the prawns are cooking, prepare the spinach leaves. Wash the leaves thoroughly, blanch them for 30 seconds in boiling water, then refresh them under cold running water and drain well. Remove the central rib from each leaf and fold the leaf lengthwise to form a ribbon about half as wide as the length of a prawn.

As soon as the prawns are cooked, rinse them under cold running water. Twist off the heads, legs and front claws, and discard. Using a sharp pair of scissors, slit the underside of the shell along the belly of the shellfish, up to the tail fins. Using a sharp knife, remove the dark vein. Remove most of the shell, leaving only the tail fins intact.

Combine the soy sauce and mirin in a small bowl, and dip each prawn in the mixture. Wrap the end opposite the tail in a spinach leaf ribbon, leaving the tail fins and a little of the body exposed. (The spinach will adhere to itself.)

Arrange the prawns on a serving dish. Serve the remaining soy sauce and mirin mixture as a dip and, for those who like hot food, serve the wasabi powder in a separate bowl.

Smoked Salmon Roll-Ups

Makes 16 roll-ups
Working (and total) time: about 30 minutes

Per roll-up:			
Calories **30**	16	baby sweetcorn	16
Protein **3g**	15 g	dill, finely chopped	½ oz
Cholesterol **5mg**		freshly ground black pepper	
Total fat **1g**	60 g	fromage frais	2 oz
Saturated fat **trace**	125 g	smoked salmon, cut into 16 thin strips about 7.5 by 5 cm (3 by 2 inches) each	4 oz
Sodium **180mg**	16	chives or slivers of spring onion	16
		lime wedges, for garnish	

Pour enough water into a saucepan to fill it about 2.5 cm (1 inch) deep. Set a vegetable steamer in the pan and bring the water to the boil. Put the sweetcorn in the steamer and steam until just soft — about 5 minutes. Remove from the steamer and allow to cool.

Blend the dill and some freshly ground black pepper into the *fromage frais*, and spread each strip of smoked salmon with a little of this mixture. Roll a strip of salmon round each baby sweetcorn, and tie a chive or spring onion sliver round the salmon. Arrange on a serving dish and garnish with the lime wedges.

EDITOR'S NOTE: *Smoked salmon trout may be substituted for the smoked salmon in this recipe.*

Sushi of Prawn and Seaweed Wrapped in Radicchio

THIS RECIPE CALLS FOR WAKAME, A GREEN SEAWEED COMMON IN JAPAN. SOLD DRIED BY HEALTH FOOD SHOPS AND JAPANESE GROCERIES, IT MUST BE SOAKED BRIEFLY BEFORE USE.

Makes 24 sushi
Working time: about 30 minutes
Total time: about 1 hour and 20 minutes

Per sushi:
Calories **40**
Protein **1g**
Cholesterol **5mg**
Total fat **trace**
Saturated fat **trace**
Sodium **75mg**

200 g	sushi rice	7 oz
1 tsp	salt	1 tsp
2 tsp	sugar	2 tsp
2 tbsp	rice vinegar, plus 1 tsp	2 tbsp
24	chives, or two spring onions cut into very fine ribbons	24
90 g	shelled cooked prawns	3 oz
⅛ tsp	wasabi powder	⅛ tsp
1 ½ tsp	dried wakame	1 ½ tsp
12	large radicchio leaves	12

Put the rice in a large bowl and add about five times its volume of water. Stir gently, then carefully pour off the water. Repeat the rinsing twice, then drain the rice and leave it in a sieve for about 45 minutes to allow the grains to absorb any residual water.

Put the rice in a saucepan with ¼ litre (8 fl oz) of water and bring to the boil, partially covered, over high heat. Reduce the heat to very low, cover the pan and simmer for 10 minutes. Leave the pan on the stove, with the heat turned off, for 10 to 15 minutes. Dissolve the salt and sugar in 2 tablespoons of the vinegar, and mix into the rice with a wet wooden spoon.

While the rice is being prepared, blanch the chives or spring onions by pouring boiling water over them in a deep bowl. Refresh them immediately in cold water, drain, then lay out on paper towels to dry. Devein and dice the prawns. Mix the wasabi powder with a little water to make a paste. Soak the wakame in water for 5 to 10 minutes (it will quadruple in size), then squeeze it dry in a tea towel.

Cut each radicchio leaf in half lengthwise and trim away the thick, white centre ribs. Mix the remaining teaspoon of vinegar with 3 tablespoons of water in a small bowl; dip your fingers in the bowl and spread the rice over three quarters of the length of each leaf with your fingers, pressing it down. Spread a thin layer of wasabi paste over the rice, followed by the wakame, and then the prawns.

Roll up each leaf to enclose the rice and filling, wrapping the empty quarter of the leaf neatly round the roll. Tie a ribbon of chive or spring onion round each sushi to secure it, and trim the sides with a sharp knife to neaten. Arrange the sushi on serving plates.

EDITOR'S NOTE: *Italian short-grain rice may be used instead of sushi rice. Dry mustard may be substituted for wasabi.*

Lemon and Tarragon Scallop Croustades

Makes 24 croustades
Working time: about 20 minutes
Total time: about 30 minutes

Per croustade:
Calories **20**
Protein **1g**
Cholesterol **5mg**
Total fat **1g**
Saturated fat **0g**
Sodium **45mg**

6	slices wholemeal bread	6
15 g	polyunsaturated margarine, melted	½ oz
	Lemon and tarragon filling	
6	scallops, bright white connective tissue removed, liquor from shells reserved	6
4 tsp	arrowroot	4 tsp
½ tsp	grated lemon rind	½ tsp
½ tsp	fresh lemon juice	½ tsp
1 tsp	finely chopped fresh tarragon	1 tsp
	freshly ground black pepper	
1 tsp	single cream	1 tsp
	fresh tarragon sprigs, for garnish	
	thin strips of lemon rind, for garnish	

Preheat the oven to 220°C (425°F or Mark 7).
To make the cases, flatten the slices of bread with a rolling pin. Using a 6 cm (2½ inch) daisy-shaped cutter, cut out 24 shapes. Brush 24 small bun tins, about 4 cm (1½ inches) in diameter, with some of the margarine, and press the bread into the moulds. Brush the bread cases with the remaining margarine, and bake them in the oven until they are browned and crisp — about 10 minutes. Set aside to cool.

To prepare the filling, strain the liquor from the scallop shells into a measuring jug, and make up to 15 cl (¼ pint) with cold water. Place the arrowroot in a small bowl and blend it with 2 tablespoons of the liquid.

Pour the remaining liquid into a small saucepan and bring it to the boil; add the scallops and simmer, covered, for 2 minutes. Remove the scallops with a slotted spoon, dice them and set aside.

Pour the arrowroot mixture into the liquid and stir. Add the grated lemon rind and juice, tarragon and some pepper. Bring to the boil and cook for 1 minute, then remove the pan from the heat and stir in the cream and scallops.

Arrange the bread cases on a serving plate. Divide the filling among them, and garnish with the tarragon sprigs and lemon rind. Serve at room temperature.

Stuffed Squid Rings

Makes 32 rings
Working time: about 30 minutes
Total time: about 1 hour 15 minutes

Per ring:
Calories **15**
Protein **3g**
Cholesterol **35mg**
Total fat **trace**
Saturated fat **trace**
Sodium **25mg**

8	small young squid (about 500 g/1 lb), cleaned and skinned (opposite page)	8
8	leaves red lollo or other crisp lettuce, washed and dried	8
100 g	turbot or halibut, skinned and diced	3½ oz

30 cl	unsalted fish or vegetable stock (recipes, page 139)	½ pint
2 tbsp	low-sodium soy sauce or shoyu	2 tbsp
2.5 cm	piece fresh ginger root, finely sliced	1 inch
1 tbsp	molasses	1 tbsp
1 tbsp	balsamic vinegar, or ½ tbsp red wine vinegar	1 tbsp

Drain and dry the squid tentacles and pouches with paper towels. Spread open a lettuce leaf and trim it to the same length as one of the pouches. Place a set of tentacles along the centre line of the leaf and arrange an eighth of the diced fish on the leaf at the tentacle tips. Roll up the leaf tightly and place the lettuce package inside one of the pouches. Trim away any excess leaf and secure the pouch opening with a cocktail stick. Stuff the remaining pouches in the same way.

Combine the stock, soy sauce, ginger, molasses and vinegar in a saucepan or fireproof casserole, and bring to the boil. Add the stuffed squid, cover and simmer gently until the squid are tender — 30 to 45 minutes. As both the squid and the lettuce will shrink considerably, releasing juices as they cook, turning should not be necessary, but check occasionally that all surfaces are covered by liquid and add more water if they are not. Allow the squid to cool in their liquid, then chill in the refrigerator.

Shortly before serving, drain the squid and remove the cocktail sticks. Slice each pouch into four rings.

SUGGESTED ACCOMPANIMENT: *small crisp lettuce leaves, for easy handling.*

Preparing a Squid for Cooking

1 *SEPARATING THE POUCH AND TENTACLES. Working over a bowl of water or a sink, hold the squid's pouch in one hand and its tentacles in the other. Gently pull the tentacles until the viscera separate from the inside of the pouch. Place the tentacles, with the head and viscera still attached, in the bowl.*

2 *REMOVING THE PEN. Feel inside the pouch with your fingers to locate the pen, or quill — a cartilaginous structure running nearly the length of the pouch. Pull out the pen and discard it. Reach inside the pouch again and scrape out any remaining gelatinous material with your fingers; wash the pouch thoroughly.*

3 *SKINNING THE POUCH. Carefully pull off the edible triangular fins on either side of the pouch and skin them. Starting at the open end of the pouch, use your fingers to pull the mottled purplish skin away from the pale flesh. Continue peeling off the skin from the pouch; discard the skin. Rinse the pouch and wings, then set aside in a bowl of fresh cold water.*

4 *CUTTING OFF THE TENTACLES. Lay the viscera, head and tentacles on a cutting board. Sever the tentacles from the head below the eyes; the tentacles should remain joined together by a narrow band of flesh. Discard the head and viscera. If any of the bony beak remains in the tentacle section, squeeze it out.*

Roulade of Salmon and Sole Filled with Spinach

Makes about 35 slices
Working time: about 45 minutes
Total time: about 4 hours (includes chilling)

Per slice:
Calories **30**
Protein **4g**
Cholesterol **15mg**
Total fat **2g**
Saturated fat **trace**
Sodium **70mg**

350 g	middle cut salmon	12 oz
300 g	Dover sole or plaice fillets, skinned	10 oz
350 g	spinach, washed and stemmed	12 oz
1	lemon, roughly sliced	1
1	onion, roughly chopped	1
2	carrots, roughly sliced	2
2 tsp	black peppercorns	2 tsp
30 g	parsley sprigs	1 oz
45 cl	white wine vinegar	¾ pint
1 tsp	chopped fresh dill	1 tsp
1 tsp	salt	1 tsp
2.5 litres	unsalted fish stock (recipe, page 139), or water	4 pints

Cut the salmon in half lengthwise and remove all the bones; trim any membrane. Using a sharp, thin-bladed knife, cut thin horizontal slices from each half, working towards the skin. In the centre of a piece of wet muslin about 50 by 30 cm (20 by 12 inches), lay the slices of salmon to form a rectangle measuring 35 by 20 cm (14 by 8 inches); fill any gaps with odd bits of salmon. Slice the sole in the same way and lay the slices on top of the salmon to cover it completely.

Plunge the spinach into a pan of boiling water, bring back to the boil and cook for 1 minute. Drain the spinach, squeeze out as much water as possible and chop roughly. Arrange the spinach along one long edge of the fish rectangle in the shape of a cylinder about 2 cm (¾ inch) in diameter.

With both hands, grip the edge of the muslin nearest the spinach. Pull the muslin towards you and gently lift it, a little at a time, gradually rolling the fish round the spinach. Continue lifting and rolling until the roll is complete. Wrap the muslin round the completed roll and secure it at each end with string. Tie 2.5 cm (1 inch) wide strips of muslin round the roll at intervals of about 5 cm (2 inches).

To prepare a court-bouillon, place the lemon, onion, carrots, peppercorns, parsley, vinegar, dill and salt in a fish kettle or roasting pan long enough to accommodate the salmon roll. Add fish stock to a depth of about 7.5 cm (3 inches) so that the roll will be completely covered when it is put in the pan. Bring the stock to the boil, then reduce the heat until it is just simmering. Carefully place the muslin-wrapped roll in the court-bouillon and poach for 3 to 4 minutes. Take the fish kettle or pan off the heat and leave to cool. When cool, place in the refrigerator to chill thoroughly — at least 3 hours.

Carefully remove the muslin-wrapped roll from the pan and cut away the string and the muslin strips. Just before serving, unwrap the roll, taking care not to break the fish, and cut it into 1 cm (½ inch) slices. Arrange the slices on a serving plate.

Mixed Seafood Pâté

Serves 20
Working time: about 45 minutes
Total time: about 3 hours (includes marinating)

Calories **45**
Protein **7g**
Cholesterol **70mg**
Total fat **1g**
Saturated fat **1g**
Sodium **200mg**

250 g	smoked cod or haddock	8 oz
½	lime, juice squeezed, rind grated (optional)	½
30 cl	unsalted fish stock (recipe, page 139), or water with two bay leaves, six peppercorns and 2 tbsp white wine vinegar added	½ pint
250 g	cod or haddock, skinned and boned	8 oz
125 g	soft herring roe	4 oz
½ tsp	light sesame oil	½ tsp
30 g	smoked cod's roe, skinned	1 oz
1 tbsp	chopped fresh dill, plus one dill sprig for garnish	1 tbsp
2 tbsp	anise-flavoured spirit	2 tbsp
2 tbsp	fromage frais or thick Greek yogurt	2 tbsp
2 tbsp	crème fraîche or soured cream	2 tbsp
¼ tsp	cayenne pepper	¼ tsp
	paprika	
	white pepper	
1 tsp	canned green peppercorns, crushed (optional)	1 tsp
2	lime slices, for garnish	2

Skin and roughly chop the smoked fish into 5 cm (2 inch) pieces. Place the pieces in a shallow non-reactive dish, pour the lime juice over them and leave to marinate for about 2 hours.

Meanwhile, bring the stock or flavoured water to the boil in a small pan, then simmer the fresh fish gently in the liquid until it flakes easily — 3 to 5 minutes. Remove the fish from the pan with a slotted spoon and set aside to cool.

Wipe the soft roe with paper towels, discarding any dark veining or blood. In a small, non-stick frying pan, gently fry the soft roe in the sesame oil for 3 to 5 minutes, breaking up the roe gently as it cooks. Set aside to cool.

Drain the marinade from the smoked fish and flake the flesh. Discard the marinade liquid. Reserve about one quarter of the fish, and place the rest in a blender or food processor. Flake the poached fish, reserve one quarter and place the rest in the blender or food processor. Add the soft and smoked roes, and process the mixture briefly. Add the dill, anise-flavoured spirit, *fromage frais*, *crème fraîche*, the cayenne pepper, some paprika and some white pepper together with the grated lime rind and green peppercorns, if you are using them, and blend the mixture until smooth. Stir in the reserved flaked fish.

Spoon the seafood pâté into a serving dish. Garnish the top with a sprinkling of paprika, the lime slices and the dill sprig.

SUGGESTED ACCOMPANIMENT: *Melba toast (page 11).*

Minced Lamb and Burghul

KNOWN AS *KIBBEH NAYEH* IN ARAB COUNTRIES, THIS DISH OF RAW MEAT AND BURGHUL ORIGINATED IN TURKEY. IT IS ALWAYS MADE WITH VERY LEAN LAMB.

Makes about 30 discs
Working (and total) time: about 20 minutes

Per 3 discs:
Calories **175**
Protein **18g**
Cholesterol **35mg**
Total fat **5g**
Saturated fat **2g**
Sodium **150mg**

500 g	lean lamb for mincing, trimmed of all fat	1 lb
250 g	fine-grade burghul	8 oz
1	large onion, grated	1
1 tsp	ground cumin	1 tsp
1 ½ tsp	cayenne pepper	1 ½ tsp
1 tsp	salt	1 tsp
	freshly ground black pepper	
4	spring onions, finely chopped	4
2 tbsp	finely chopped parsley	2 tbsp
	small leaves of crisp lettuce	

Pass the meat three times through the fine blade of a mincer. Put the burghul in a large bowl, pour boiling water over it and leave it to stand for 2 minutes. Drain the burghul in a sieve and rinse it under cold running water; scoop up handfuls and squeeze out excess water, returning the squeezed-out burghul to the bowl as you proceed.

Combine the minced meat, grated onion, cumin and cayenne pepper in a food processor to make a coarse paste. Tip the paste into the bowl of burghul, add the salt and some freshly ground black pepper, and knead for at least 10 minutes to thoroughly mix all the ingredients; add about 2 tablespoons of cold water while kneading to moisten the mixture.

When the paste is smooth, mix in the finely chopped spring onions and the parsley. Make about 30 little balls, then flatten these with your thumb into small discs. Serve the discs on individual lettuce leaves for eating with the fingers.

Rabbit Terrine

THIS LIGHT, MOIST TERRINE MAY BE SERVED IN SLICES OR CUT
UP AS BITE-SIZED PIECES.

Makes 12 slices
Working time: about 30 minutes
Total time: about 6 hours (includes chilling)

Per slice:
Calories **100**
Protein **12g**
Cholesterol **40mg**
Total fat **4g**
Saturated fat **2g**
Sodium **120mg**

15 g	unsalted butter	½ oz
1	onion, finely chopped	1
15 g	plain flour	½ oz
2	bay leaves	2
4	cloves	4
30 cl	light ale	½ pint
½ tsp	salt	½ tsp
	freshly ground black pepper	
500 g	boned rabbit, finely minced	1 lb
175 g	lean pork fillet, finely minced	6 oz
1 tsp	honey	1 tsp
1 tbsp	cranberries	1 tbsp
	watercress leaves, washed and dried, for garnish	

Preheat the oven to 170°C (325°F or Mark 3). Line the
base and sides of a 1 kg (2 lb) loaf tin with foil.

Melt the butter in a heavy-bottomed saucepan over
medium heat, add the onion and cook for 1 minute,
stirring occasionally. Stir in the flour, bay leaves,
cloves, light ale, salt and some pepper. Bring to the
boil, stirring, and cook gently for 2 minutes. Remove
the pan from the heat; discard the bay leaves and
cloves, and stir in the rabbit and pork.

Pour the terrine mixture into the prepared tin and
smooth the top. Cover with a double thickness of foil.
Stand the tin in a larger pan, and pour water into the
pan until it comes half way up the sides of the loaf tin.
Bake in the centre of the oven until the terrine is
firm — about 1½ hours.

Remove the tin from the water, loosen the foil and
place a heavy weight on top of the terrine. Leave in the
refrigerator for 4 to 5 hours, or overnight.

Put the honey in a small saucepan with 1 tablespoon of cold water, bring to the boil, then reduce the
heat. Add the cranberries and cook for just 1 minute to
soften them; do not allow the berries to burst. Remove
the berries with a slotted spoon and place on paper
towels. Leave to dry.

To serve, turn the terrine out on to a plate, garnish
with the cranberries and watercress leaves, and cut
into slices or tiny squares.

SUGGESTED ACCOMPANIMENT: *dry biscuits or toast.*

Pork Sticks with Tomato and Fennel Sauce

Makes about 40 sticks
Working time: about 30 minutes
Total time: about 1 hour and 20 minutes

Per stick:
Calories **30**
Protein **2g**
Cholesterol **30mg**
Total fat **2g**
Saturated fat **1g**
Sodium **30mg**

400 g	pork fillet in one piece, trimmed of fat	14 oz
2 tsp	virgin olive oil	2 tsp
½ tsp	fennel seeds, lightly crushed	½ tsp
¼ tsp	salt	¼ tsp
	freshly ground black pepper	
350 g	bulb fennel, feathery tops chopped, bulbs halved	12 oz
1	thick lemon slice	1
Tomato and fennel sauce		
2 tbsp	virgin olive oil	2 tbsp
1	garlic clove, finely chopped	1
250 g	bulb fennel, trimmed and coarsely chopped	8 oz
½ tsp	fennel seeds, lightly crushed	½ tsp
½	orange, pared rind only	½
4 tbsp	anise-flavoured spirit	4 tbsp
500 g	tomatoes, skinned, seeded (page 76) and chopped	1 lb
¼ tsp	salt	¼ tsp
	freshly ground black pepper	
	pared orange rind, julienned, for garnish	

Preheat the oven to 230°C (450°F or Mark 8). Brush the pork fillet lightly with the oil and rub it with the crushed fennel seeds. Roast the pork for 20 to 25 minutes, then season with the salt and a little pepper, wrap loosely in foil and leave to cool.

Meanwhile, make the tomato and fennel sauce. Heat the oil in a sauté pan and cook the garlic gently for a minute or two. Stir in the chopped fennel, crushed fennel seeds, pared orange rind, anise-flavoured spirit and some freshly ground pepper. Cover and simmer for 10 minutes. Add the chopped tomatoes and simmer for a further 10 minutes; allow the mixture to cool. Discard the orange rind, then blend the sauce in a food processor. Add the salt and set aside.

Parboil the halved fennel bulbs together with the lemon slice for about 5 minutes, or until the fennel is just tender. Drain, and discard the lemon; refresh the fennel under cold running water and drain well. Cut the fennel into about forty 1 cm (½ inch) cubes.

Unwrap the cooled fillet and cut it lengthwise into strips, then slice across to give about forty 2 cm (¾ inch) cubes. Thread cocktail sticks with one piece of fennel and one of pork. Dip the sticks in the chopped fennel tops and arrange them on a dish. Serve the sauce separately, garnished with the julienned orange rind.

Pork and Cheese Canapés with Apricot Chutney

Makes 36 canapés
Working time: about 20 minutes
Total time: about 12 hours (includes soaking)

Per pork canapé:			
Calories **35**	125 g	lean cold roast pork, cubed	4 oz
Protein **2g**	36	Melba toasts (page 11) or dry biscuits, approximately 4 cm (1 ½ inches) square	36
Cholesterol **5mg**			
Total fat **1g**	4	kumquats, thinly sliced	4
Saturated fat **0g**		flat-leaf parsley	
Sodium **20mg**	90 g	medium-fat curd cheese	3 oz
	Apricot chutney		
Per cheese canapé:	60 g	dried apricots, soaked in boiling water for 12 hours	2 oz
Calories **45**			
Protein **2g**	20 g	set honey	¾ oz
Cholesterol **5mg**	1 tbsp	cider vinegar	1 tbsp
Total fat **3g**	1 cm	piece fresh root ginger, peeled and finely chopped	½ inch
Saturated fat **0g**			
Sodium **50mg**	1 cm	slice stem ginger, finely chopped	½ inch
	¼ tsp	ground cinnamon	¼ tsp
	⅛ tsp	ground allspice	⅛ tsp
	⅛ tsp	salt	⅛ tsp

To make the chutney, drain the apricots and purée them with the honey in a food processor. Add the vinegar, root and stem ginger, cinnamon, allspice and salt, and blend to amalgamate thoroughly. Put the chutney in a bowl or jar.

Mince the pork in a food processor until it binds together. Add about two thirds of the chutney and blend to form a smooth paste.

Spread the meat and chutney paste over half of the toasts or biscuits, and garnish each with a slice of kumquat and a parsley leaf. Spread the curd cheese over the remaining biscuits, and top each with half a teaspoon of the remaining chutney. Arrange the canapés on a serving plate.

EDITOR'S NOTE: *Any excess chutney may be kept in the refrigerator for up to a fortnight.*

Vegetable Aspic

TO MAKE A CLEAR VEGETABLE ASPIC, THE BOWLS AND COOKING
UTENSILS MUST BE SCRUPULOUSLY CLEAN. HERE, EVERYTHING
IS SCALDED TO ENSURE THAT THE LIQUID DOES NOT BECOME
CLOUDED BY IMPURITIES.

Makes about 90 cl (1½ pints)
Working time: about 45 minutes
Total time: about 2 hours and 45 minutes

Per total recipe:
Calories **410**
Protein **53g**
Cholesterol **0mg**
Total fat **trace**
Saturated fat **0g**
Sodium **1,480mg**

250 g	carrots, sliced	8 oz
250 g	leeks, sliced	8 oz
2	onions, finely chopped	2
4	sticks celery, sliced	4
1	small bunch parsley	1
1	rosemary sprig	1
1	thyme sprig	1
4	garlic cloves, unpeeled	4
½ tsp	salt	½ tsp
8	black peppercorns	8
45 g	powdered gelatine	1½ oz
2	eggs, whites only, washed shells reserved	2
1 tbsp	red wine vinegar	1 tbsp

Put the carrots, leeks, onions, celery, parsley,
rosemary, thyme, garlic, salt and peppercorns into a
large saucepan with 1.75 litres (3 pints) of cold water.
Bring to the boil, then reduce the heat and partially
cover the saucepan with a lid. Simmer gently for about

2 hours, or until the liquid is reduced by half.

Strain the stock through a nylon sieve into a large bowl; discard the vegetables. Measure the stock, and make up to 90 cl (1½ pints) with water, if necessary.

Rinse the saucepan and fill it with cold water. Put a wire whisk, a large metal sieve and a large square of muslin into the saucepan. Bring the water to the boil. Remove the whisk, sieve and muslin from the pan; pour the boiling water into a large bowl to scald it, then pour the water away. Place the sieve over the bowl and line the sieve with the muslin.

Pour the stock back into the saucepan and add the gelatine, egg whites and shells, and vinegar. With the scalded whisk, whisk the stock over moderate heat until the egg whites form a thick foam on the surface.

Stop whisking, then bring the mixture to the boil so that the foam rises to the top of the saucepan — do not allow it to boil over. Remove the saucepan from the heat and allow the foam to settle back down. Repeat this process twice more, then allow the mixture to stand for 5 minutes.

Very gently and carefully pour the aspic through the lined sieve, without allowing the foam floating on top of the liquid to break up. Leave to drain thoroughly, then let the aspic cool. Once it has cooled, the aspic sets to a jelly-like consistency.

Vegetable aspic may be kept in the refrigerator for a few days, ready to be used when needed. Once set, it can be quickly melted again by placing the bowl over a saucepan of hot water.

Asparagus Canapés

Makes 12 canapés
Working time: about 45 minutes
Total time: about 1 hour and 10 minutes (includes setting)

12	asparagus spears	12
3 or 4	thin slices rye bread	3 or 4
½	sweet red pepper, skinned (page 22), seeded and deribbed	½
20 g	polyunsaturated margarine	¾ oz
1	small garlic clove, crushed	1
1 tbsp	finely chopped parsley	1 tbsp
⅛ tsp	salt	⅛ tsp
	freshly ground black pepper	
15 cl	vegetable aspic (recipe, left), melted	¼ pint

Per canapé:
Calories **30**
Protein **1g**
Cholesterol **0mg**
Total fat **2g**
Saturated fat **trace**
Sodium **60mg**

Trim the asparagus, then carefully peel each stalk up to the tip. Cook the spears in boiling water until they are tender — 5 to 6 minutes — then drain in a colander and refresh them under cold running water. Drain the asparagus well.

Trim the crusts from the rye bread, then cut the slices into 12 oblongs measuring about 6 by 3 cm (2½ by 1¼ inches).

Trim the asparagus tip to the length of the bread oblongs, then slice each tip in half lengthwise. (Use the stalks for a salad.) Cut the red pepper into thin strips, about the same length as the asparagus pieces.

Put the margarine, garlic, parsley, salt and some pepper into a small bowl. Beat until smooth, then spread thinly over the rye bread.

Place two asparagus tip halves on each piece of bread and drape a strip of red pepper across the asparagus. Put the canapés on a wire rack, placed over a large tray. Stir the aspic over ice, or refrigerate, until it begins to thicken. Carefully spoon the aspic over the canapés to coat them evenly, then refrigerate until firmly set — about 20 minutes. Keep the canapés refrigerated until just before serving.

Seafood Canapés

Makes 12 canapés
Working time: about 1 hour
Total time: about 2 hours and 30 minutes
(includes cooling and setting)

175 g	haddock fillet	6 oz
1	egg white	1
⅜ tsp	salt	⅜ tsp
90 g	thick Greek yogurt	3 oz
	freshly ground black pepper	
3 or 4	thin slices wholemeal bread, toasted	3 or 4
15 g	polyunsaturated margarine	½ oz
½ tsp	tomato paste	½ tsp
2 tsp	finely chopped basil leaves	2 tsp
15 cl	vegetable aspic (recipe, left), melted	¼ pint
12	peeled cooked prawns	12
3 tsp	black caviare or lump fish roe	3 tsp

Per canapé:
Calories **40**
Protein **2g**
Cholesterol **30mg**
Total fat **2g**
Saturated fat **trace**
Sodium **110mg**

Rinse the haddock fillet under cold running water and pat it dry with paper towels. Carefully remove the skin from the haddock, then remove any bones and cut the fish roughly into cubes. Put the haddock into a food processor or blender with the egg white and ¼ tsp of the salt, and blend to a smooth paste. Work the paste through a nylon sieve into a bowl to remove any coarse sinews. Cover the bowl and refrigerate the mixture for 30 minutes.

Meanwhile, grease 12 tiny, differently shaped *petits fours* moulds. Pour enough water into a saucepan to fill it about 2.5 cm (1 inch) deep, set a steamer in the pan and bring the water to the boil.

▶

Remove the chilled fish mixture from the refrigerator. Gradually beat in the yogurt, and season with some black pepper. Fill the prepared moulds with the fish mousse. Place the moulds in the steamer and cover them closely with a sheet of non-stick parchment paper; steam until the mousse is firm — 1½ to 2 minutes. Remove the moulds from the steamer and refrigerate until quite cold.

Using a 4 cm (1¾ inch) plain round cutter, cut 12 rounds from the toast. Put the margarine, tomato paste, basil, the remaining salt and a little pepper into a bowl, and beat together until smooth. Spread the mixture thinly over each round of toast.

Carefully unmould the haddock mousses. Dip each mousse, balanced on a fork, in the vegetable aspic, and place it on a round of toast. Put the canapés on a wire rack over a tray, and refrigerate them for about 5 minutes to set the aspic. Dip the peeled prawns in the aspic and place one prawn neatly on each canapé. Refrigerate for 5 minutes to set the aspic.

Stir the remaining aspic over ice, or refrigerate, until it begins to thicken. Carefully spoon the aspic over the canapés to coat them evenly. Immediately, spoon a little caviare on to each one. Refrigerate for about 20 minutes to set firmly. Keep the canapés refrigerated until just before serving.

EDITOR'S NOTE: *The haddock mousses may be made the day before and kept in the refrigerator.*

Duck Canapés

Makes 12 canapés
Working time: about 45 minutes
Total time: about 2 hours and 15 minutes
(includes cooling and setting)

Per canapé:
Calories **105**
Protein **8g**
Cholesterol **35mg**
Total fat **4g**
Saturated fat **1g**
Sodium **80mg**

1 tbsp	virgin olive oil	1 tbsp
500 g	boned duck breasts, skinned	1 lb
15 g	plain flour	½ oz
15 cl	unsalted chicken stock (recipe, page 139)	¼ pint
1	small sweet red pepper, skinned, (page 22), seeded, deribbed and puréed	1
¼ tsp	salt	¼ tsp
	white pepper	
15 cl	vegetable aspic (recipe, page 50), melted	¼ pint
2 tsp	clear honey	2 tsp
12	thin slices kumquat	12
6	cranberries	6
6	thin slices rye bread	6
15 g	polyunsaturated margarine	½ oz

Heat the oil in a small heavy frying pan over medium heat. Place the duck breasts in the pan and lightly brown both sides to seal them. Reduce the heat to low, then place a flat plate on top of the breasts to prevent them from curling up. Cook gently for 20 to 25 minutes, until the duck is tender and the juices run clear when it is pierced with a skewer; turn the breasts over half way through cooking. Using a slotted spoon, transfer the duck to a plate; cover with another, flat plate and place a heavy weight (about 500 g/1 lb) on top. Set aside to cool.

Meanwhile, stir the flour into the duck juices remaining in the pan, then gradually add the stock. Bring to the boil, stirring continuously until the sauce thickens, then reduce the heat and simmer for 5 minutes, stirring occasionally. Remove the pan from the heat and stir 2 tablespoons of the sweet pepper purée into the sauce (any remaining pepper purée will not be needed). Season the sauce with the salt and some pepper, then stir in 3 tablespoons of the aspic. Cover the surface of the sauce closely with plastic film to prevent a skin from forming, and set it aside to cool.

Meanwhile, heat the honey and 1 tablespoon of cold water together in a small saucepan until boiling, then reduce the heat. Add the kumquat slices and cook gently for 1 minute, to soften slightly. Using a slotted spoon, carefully lift the slices on to paper towels to drain. Add the cranberries to the remaining syrup and cook for no more than 1 minute, just long enough to soften them; take care not to let the berries burst. Drain them on paper towels, then cut each cranberry in half lengthwise.

Cut the duck breasts horizontally into thin slices. Then, using a 6 by 3.5 cm (2½ by 1⅜ inch) oval cutter, cut out 12 shapes and place them on a wire rack over a large tray. (If necessary, ends of slices may be placed side by side and then cut into shape — the joins will be concealed by the sauce and garnish.)

When the sauce is just beginning to set, spoon it over the duck ovals. Refrigerate for 10 to 15 minutes to set the aspic firmly.

With a sharp knife cut out 12 ovals from the rye bread, using the non-cutting, slightly larger edge of the cutter as a template. Spread each shape with the margarine. Carefully lift the coated breasts from the rack and place each one on an oval of rye bread. Place these on a clean rack over a clean tray. Dip the kumquat slices and cranberry halves in the aspic and arrange them neatly on the duck canapés. Refrigerate for 5 minutes to set the aspic.

Stir the remaining aspic over ice, or refrigerate, until just beginning to set, then spoon over each canapé to coat evenly. Refrigerate for 20 to 30 minutes to set firmly. Keep refrigerated until ready to serve.

EDITOR'S NOTE: *The duck may be cooked up to one day in advance and kept in the refrigerator until required.*

Chicken Canapés

Makes 12 canapés
Working time: about 1 hour
Total time: about 2 hours and 30 minutes
(includes cooling and setting)

Per canapé:
Calories **100**
Protein **10g**
Cholesterol **25mg**
Total fat **4g**
Saturated fat **1g**
Sodium **125mg**

500 g	boned chicken breasts, skinned	1 lb
1	small onion	1
1	stick celery, roughly chopped	1
1	small carrot, roughly chopped	1
1	parsley sprig	1
1	bay leaf	1
⅜ tsp	salt	⅜ tsp
4	black peppercorns	4
30 cl	unsalted chicken stock (recipe, page 139)	½ pint
35 g	polyunsaturated margarine	1¼ oz
35 g	plain flour	1¼ oz
2 tbsp	fromage frais	2 tbsp
15 cl	vegetable aspic (recipe, page 50), melted	¼ pint
3 or 4	thin slices wholemeal bread, toasted	3 or 4
1	small garlic clove, crushed	1
1 tbsp	finely chopped parsley	1 tbsp
	freshly ground black pepper	
½	sweet red pepper, skinned (page 22), seeded and deribbed	½
	strips of cucumber skin	

Put the chicken breasts into a saucepan with the onion, celery, carrot, parsley, bay leaf, ¼ teaspoon of the salt, the peppercorns and stock. Bring to the boil, then reduce the heat and cover the saucepan with a tightly fitting lid. Simmer gently until the chicken breasts are just cooked — 5 to 6 minutes. Allow to cool, then remove the chicken breasts from the stock and refrigerate until quite cold.

Strain the stock and reserve 15 cl (¼ pint) — the rest of the stock will not be needed. Melt 15 g (½ oz) of the margarine in a saucepan and stir in the flour. Gradually add the reserved stock and bring to the boil, stirring all the time until the sauce thickens. Reduce the heat and simmer for 4 to 5 minutes, stirring occasionally. Remove from the heat and allow to cool slightly. Whisk the *fromage frais* and 3 tablespoons of the aspic into the sauce. Cover the surface of the sauce closely with plastic film to prevent a skin from forming, and refrigerate until the sauce begins to thicken — 20 to 30 minutes.

Carefully cut each chicken breast horizontally into 5 mm (¼ inch) thick slices. Using a 5 cm (2 inch) heart-shaped cutter, cut out 12 hearts from the slices of chicken. (If necessary, ends of slices may be placed side by side and then cut into shape — the joins will be concealed by the sauce and garnish.)

Place the hearts on a wire rack over a large tray. Spoon the sauce over the hearts and refrigerate for about 20 minutes, until set.

Using a 6 cm (2¼ inch) heart-shaped cutter, cut out 12 hearts from the toast. Put the remaining margarine into a small bowl with the garlic, parsley, the remaining salt and some pepper. Beat together until smooth, then spread thinly over each toast heart. Lift the coated chicken pieces from the rack and put one piece on each toast heart. Place them on a clean rack over a clean tray.

Using a small aspic cutter, cut out petal shapes from the red pepper and the cucumber skin. Dip the petals in the aspic and place them on the chicken hearts. Refrigerate for about 5 minutes to set. Stir the remaining aspic over ice, or refrigerate, until just beginning to thicken. Carefully spoon the aspic over the canapés to coat them evenly. Chill for about 20 minutes, until firmly set. Keep refrigerated until just before serving.

EDITOR'S NOTE: *The chicken may be cooked up to a day in advance and kept in the refrigerator until required.*

Egg and Watercress Canapés

Makes 12 canapés
Working time: about 30 minutes
Total time: about 1 hour and 15 minutes
(includes cooling and setting)

Per canapé:
Calories **35**
Protein **2g**
Cholesterol **40mg**
Total fat **2g**
Saturated fat **trace**
Sodium **70mg**

3	eggs	3
3 or 4	thin slices rye bread	3 or 4
15 g	polyunsaturated margarine	½ oz
1 tbsp	finely chopped watercress leaves, plus 12 whole watercress leaves	1 tbsp
⅛ tsp	salt	⅛ tsp
	freshly ground black pepper	
15 cl	vegetable aspic (recipe, page 50), melted	¼ pint

Put the eggs into a saucepan and cover with cold water. Bring to the boil, then cook them gently for 10 minutes. Immediately, pour off the boiling water and cool the eggs under cold running water. Carefully remove the shells.

Using a 4 cm (1¾ inch) diameter plain round cutter, cut 12 rounds from the rye bread. Put the margarine, chopped watercress, salt and some pepper into a small bowl. Beat until smooth, then spread thinly over each round of rye bread.

Using an egg slicer, slice the eggs. Choose the 12 best slices and place one on each round of bread. (Use the remaining slices in a salad.)

Dip each whole watercress leaf in the aspic and place one leaf on each canapé. Place the canapés on a wire rack over a large tray and refrigerate for about 5 minutes to set. Stir the remaining aspic over ice, or refrigerate, until it begins to thicken. Carefully spoon the aspic over the canapés to coat them evenly. Refrigerate until set firm — about 20 minutes. Keep the canapés refrigerated until just before serving.

2 *Mussels on the half shell coated with a fragrant tomato and fennel relish make an appealing and quickly prepared party dish (recipe, page 76).*

Hot Festive Food

With their enticing aromas and satisfying warmth, hot snacks are among the most eagerly received offerings at any gathering. But to present them when they are most welcome requires planning. For the guests' enjoyment, as well as for your own convenience, you should aim to stagger the arrival of the various dishes throughout the party.

Use the period just before the party starts to cook those dishes which have the longest cooking times. Have ready some dishes that are precooked and only need reheating; the anchovy-tomato dip *(page 66)* and the mussels on the half shell *(left)* take well to this treatment. Also prepare for the oven or pan any dishes with brief cooking times, such as lemon sole roulades *(page 85)* and veal with an apricot and nut stuffing *(page 96)*. At intervals during the party, you can then cook or reheat such dishes and bring them out piping hot. If the workload becomes overwhelming, remember that many dishes designed for eating hot are just as good served at room temperature. The cocktail quiches *(page 59)*, spicy chicken wings *(page 87)* and *pissaladière* tartlets *(page 71)*, for example, are equally delicious hot or cold.

The 46 recipes in this chapter contain many party favourites presented in a healthier guise. Popcorn *(page 57)* is flavoured with spices in place of excessive salt. High-fat puff pastry cases are discarded in favour of lower-fat alternatives such as yeast dough, paper-thin phyllo pastry and lightly oiled bread shapes. Even the sausage roll, perennially popular but notoriously fatty, is transformed beyond recognition into a slender, crisp blanket of wholemeal bread enclosing a filling of the leanest pork. Indeed, the whole genre of sausages takes on a new lease of life: gone are the mass-produced cylinders of fatty meat and gristle, replaced by light mixtures of lean beef and herbs *(page 98)*, vegetables *(page 72)* and seafood *(page 86)*.

The new, light dishes demand some new skills. To help you achieve professional results, the chapter includes step-by-step instructions for such techniques as butterflying a prawn, making tortellini and shaping triangular samosas.

Plantain Crisps

Serves 10
Working time: about 20 minutes
Total time: about 50 minutes

Calories **110**
Protein **1g**
Cholesterol **0mg**
Total fat **6g**
Saturated fat **1g**
Sodium **trace**

4	large green plantains	4
4 tbsp	safflower oil	4 tbsp

Top and tail the plantains with a stainless steel knife. Slit the skin of each plantain lengthwise into quarters, then peel off the strips of skin.

With a lightly oiled knife, slice the plantains as thinly as possible. Place the slices in a bowl of salted water and set aside for about 30 minutes, then drain them and pat them dry.

Heat the oil in a non-stick frying pan over medium heat and fry the first batch of plantain slices for 1½ to 2 minutes, turning once, until they are golden-brown. Cook the remaining slices in the same way. As each batch is cooked, remove the slices from the pan with a slotted spoon and lay them on paper towels to absorb any excess fat. Serve the plantain crisps hot, in a lined basket or on a large plate.

Fiery Chick-Peas

Serves 14
Working time: about 20 minutes
Total time: about 2 hours and 30 minutes (includes soaking)

Calories **175**
Protein **7g**
Cholesterol **0mg**
Total fat **9g**
Saturated fat **1g**
Sodium **40mg**

500 g	dried chick-peas	1 lb
6 tbsp	virgin olive oil	6 tbsp
1	garlic clove	1
1 tsp	cayenne pepper	1 tsp
¼ tsp	salt	¼ tsp

Rinse the chick-peas under cold running water. Put them in a large, heavy-bottomed saucepan and pour in enough cold water to cover them by about 5 cm (2 inches). Discard any chick-peas that float to the surface. Cover the pan, leaving the lid ajar, and bring the water to the boil; cook the chick-peas for 2 minutes. Turn off the heat, cover the pan, and leave the chick-peas to soak for at least 1 hour. (Alternatively, soak the chick-peas overnight in cold water.)

When the chick-peas finish soaking, drain them well in a colander. Return them to the pan and pour in enough water to cover them by about 5 cm (2 inches). Bring the liquid to a simmer, and cook the chick-peas over medium-low heat until they are quite tender — 45 minutes to 1 hour. (If they appear to be drying out at any point, pour in more water.) When cooked, drain the chick-peas and allow them to cool.

Dry the chick-peas thoroughly on paper towels or a clean tea towel. Heat the oil in a heavy frying pan until shimmering. Toss in the chick-peas, stir around for a few seconds, then add the garlic.

Reduce the heat to medium and sauté the chick-peas, stirring and tossing from time to time, until their skins are golden-brown — 20 to 25 minutes. If the chick-peas pop and jump, either reduce the heat slightly or cover the pan.

Tip the chick-peas on to multiple thicknesses of paper towels and roll them around to remove as much oil as possible. While still hot, put them in a bowl, add the cayenne pepper and salt, and toss well. Serve the chick-peas warm, to be eaten with the fingers.

Savoury Popcorn

Makes 3 bowls
Working time: about 15 minutes
Total time: about 20 minutes

Herb bowl:
Calories **555**
Protein **18g**
Cholesterol **40mg**
Total fat **34g**
Saturated fat **10g**
Sodium **100mg**

Spice bowl:
Calories **135**
Protein **3g**
Cholesterol **0mg**
Total fat **8g**
Saturated fat **0g**
Sodium **10mg**

Curry bowl:
Calories **70**
Protein **2g**
Cholesterol **0mg**
Total fat **trace**
Saturated fat **trace**
Sodium **15mg**

2 tsp	safflower oil	2 tsp
175 g	popping corn	6 oz
Herb flavouring		
15 g	unsalted butter	½ oz
1	garlic clove, crushed	1
1 tbsp	freshly chopped mixed herbs, such as basil, parsley and chervil	1 tbsp
2 tsp	freshly grated Parmesan cheese	2 tsp
2 tbsp	pumpkin seeds	2 tbsp
Spice flavouring		
1 tsp	dry mustard	1 tsp
1 tsp	tomato paste	1 tsp
½ tsp	Tabasco sauce	½ tsp
1 tbsp	clear honey	1 tbsp
1 tbsp	sesame seeds	1 tbsp
Curry flavouring		
1 tsp	curry powder	1 tsp
1 tsp	turmeric	1 tsp
1 tsp	fresh lemon juice	1 tsp
1 tbsp	clear honey	1 tbsp
1 tbsp	plain low-fat yogurt	1 tbsp

To prepare the herb flavouring, melt the butter in a heavy-bottomed saucepan, then add the garlic, herbs, Parmesan cheese and pumpkin seeds. Cook, stirring continuously, for 1 minute, then set aside.

For the spice flavouring, mix together in a saucepan the mustard, tomato paste, Tabasco sauce and honey. Heat gently, stirring, until the mixture comes to the boil, then set aside.

To prepare the curry flavouring, mix together in a saucepan the curry powder, turmeric, lemon juice and honey. Heat gently, stirring continuously, until the mixture boils. Remove the saucepan from the heat and stir in the yogurt.

While the flavourings are hot, heat the oil in a large, heavy-bottomed saucepan; add the popping corn and cover. Heat gently, shaking the pan, until all the corn has popped — 2 to 3 minutes; discard any unpopped corn. Tip about one third of the popcorn into each of the flavourings and stir until evenly coated. When you stir the popcorn into the spice flavouring, add also the sesame seeds. Put the popcorn into separate bowls and serve immediately, while still warm.

Buckwheat Blinis Topped with Goat Cheese

Makes about 60 blinis
Working time: about 45 minutes
Total time: about 2 hours and 30 minutes
(includes proving)

Per blini:
Calories **35**
Protein **2g**
Cholesterol **10mg**
Total fat **2g**
Saturated fat **trace**
Sodium **65mg**

35 cl	skimmed milk	12 fl oz
15 g	fresh yeast, or 7 g (¼ oz) dried yeast	½ oz
125 g	buckwheat flour	4 oz
125 g	strong plain flour	4 oz
¼ tsp	salt	¼ tsp
½ tsp	ground caraway seeds	½ tsp
½ tsp	crushed black sesame seeds	½ tsp
2 tsp	honey	2 tsp
½ tbsp	unsalted butter	½ tbsp
1	egg, separated	1
	Goat cheese topping	
250 g	soft goat cheese	8 oz
1 ½ tbsp	sesame seeds, toasted	1 ½ tbsp
1 tbsp	caraway seeds, toasted	1 tbsp
1 tbsp	poppy seeds, toasted	1 tbsp
2 tbsp	sunflower seeds, toasted	2 tbsp

Warm 2 tablespoons of the milk, blend in the fresh yeast, and leave for about 10 to 15 minutes for the yeast to activate; if using dried yeast, reconstitute according to the manufacturer's instructions.

Sift the flours and salt into a mixing bowl, stir in the caraway and sesame seeds, and make a hollow in the flour mixture. In a small pan, gently warm the remaining milk with the honey and butter until hand hot.

Remove from the heat and stir in the yeast mixture. Pour the milk and yeast mixture, together with the egg yolk, into the flour and blend with a wooden spoon, gradually incorporating the flour until the ingredients are amalgamated. Beat for a further 2 minutes. Leave in a warm place for about 1 hour until well risen and bubbly. The batter should drop easily from a teaspoon; if it is too stiff, beat in a little warm water. Whisk the egg white and fold it into the batter.

Heat a large griddle or non-stick frying pan *(box, page 86)* over medium heat until a few drops of cold water dance when sprinkled on the surface. Drop the batter a teaspoon at a time on to the griddle or frying pan, and use the back of the spoon to spread the batter into rounds about 5 cm (2 inches) in diameter. Cook the blinis until they are covered with bubbles and the undersides are quite dry and golden — 1 to 3 minutes. Flip the blinis over and cook them until the second sides are lightly browned — about 1 minute more. Wrap up each batch of blinis in a folded cloth napkin, and keep them warm in a low oven while you cook the remaining batter.

To make the topping, beat the cheese to a smooth, even texture that falls easily from a spoon. To serve, drop a half teaspoon of cheese on each blini, and sprinkle each with one type of seed.

EDITOR'S NOTE: *In place of soft goat cheese, you may substitute 125 g (4 oz) hard goat cheese blended with 125 g (4 oz) fromage frais.*

Cocktail Quiches

Makes 18 quiches
Working time: about 1 hour
Total time: about 1 hour and 20 minutes

Per spinach quiche: Calories **140** Protein **5g** Cholesterol **35mg** Total fat **9g** Saturated fat **3g** Sodium **165mg**	175 g	flour	6 oz
	⅜ tsp	salt	⅜ tsp
	90 g	polyunsaturated margarine	3 oz
	1	egg white, lightly beaten	1
	2	eggs	2
	¼ litre	skimmed milk	8 fl oz
		freshly ground black pepper	
Per asparagus quiche: Calories **120** Protein **4g** Cholesterol **30mg** Total fat **8g** Saturated fat **2g** Sodium **160mg**	60 g	Parmesan cheese, finely grated	2 oz
	Spinach filling		
	1 tbsp	virgin olive oil	1 tbsp
	½	small onion, finely chopped	½
	⅓	small sweet red pepper, chopped	⅓
	⅓	small sweet green pepper, chopped	⅓
	250 g	spinach, stalks removed, washed	8 oz
Per mackerel quiche: Calories **115** Protein **6g** Cholesterol **35mg** Total fat **7g** Saturated fat **2g** Sodium **230mg**	**Asparagus filling**		
	3	small asparagus spears, trimmed	3
	7.5 cm	piece cucumber, peeled, halved lengthwise and seeded	3 inch
	15 g	unsalted butter	½ oz
	Mackerel filling		
	60 g	smoked mackerel fillet	2 oz

To make the dough, sift the flour and ⅛ teaspoon of the salt into a bowl, then rub in the margarine until the mixture resembles fine breadcrumbs. Add the egg white and mix, with a round-bladed knife, to form a dough. Knead the dough on a lightly floured surface until smooth.

Roll out the dough thinly then, using a 10 cm (4 inch) plain round cutter, cut out rounds. Fit the rounds into 7 cm (2¾ inch) fluted tartlet tins. Trim the edges, then re-knead and re-roll the trimmings. Cut out more rounds and line more tins, continuing until you have lined 18 tins. Place the tins on baking sheets and refrigerate while you are making the three fillings.

To prepare the spinach filling, heat the oil in a small, heavy frying pan, add the onion and sweet peppers, and cook very gently for 6 to 8 minutes, until soft but not browned. Meanwhile, bring a small saucepan of water to the boil, plunge the spinach leaves into the water and bring back to the boil for 30 seconds. Drain the spinach in a colander, then rinse under cold running water to refresh it. Squeeze the spinach dry and chop finely. Put the spinach and the pepper mixture into a small bowl and set aside.

For the asparagus filling, cut the tips off the asparagus spears and slice the stalks thinly. Cook the asparagus tips and slices in a little boiling water for 2 to 3 minutes, until tender. Drain them in a colander, then refresh under cold running water. Drain well. Cut the cucumber halves in half again lengthwise, then into thin slices. Heat the butter in a small heavy-bottomed saucepan, add the cucumber and cook for 3 to 4 minutes, until softened but not browned. Set the asparagus tips aside, and put the asparagus slices and the cucumber into a small bowl.

To prepare the mackerel filling, remove the skin from the mackerel, then flake the flesh and remove the bones. Put the flesh into a small bowl and set aside.

Preheat the oven to 220°C (425°F or Mark 7). Put the eggs and milk into a bowl, and season with the remaining salt and a little pepper. Whisk lightly together, then stir in the Parmesan cheese. Divide the egg mixture equally among the three bowls of filling and mix each one well.

Fill six of the pastry-lined tins with the asparagus mixture, six with the spinach, and six with the mackerel. Cut the reserved asparagus tips in half and place a piece on each asparagus quiche. Bake the quiches in the oven until they are golden-brown and the filling is set — 20 to 25 minutes. Carefully remove the quiches from their tins to a serving plate. Serve warm.

Courgette Soufflés

Makes 40 soufflés
Working time: about 20 minutes
Total time: about 30 minutes

Per soufflé:		
Calories **10**	5	courgettes, each about 5
Protein **trace**		18 cm (7 inches) long, ends trimmed
Cholesterol **10mg**	1 tsp	polyunsaturated margarine 1 tsp
Total fat **trace**	15 g	plain flour ½ oz
Saturated fat **trace**	4 tbsp	skimmed milk 4 tbsp
Sodium **20mg**	1	egg yolk 1
	30 g	mature Cheddar cheese, grated 1 oz
	¼ tsp	Dijon mustard ¼ tsp
	¼ tsp	salt ¼ tsp
		freshly ground black pepper
	2	egg whites 2

Using a canelle knife, cut away thin, evenly spaced strips of skin from the length of each courgette to form a crimped effect. Cut each courgette into eight slices about 2 cm (¾ inch) thick. Using a small spoon, scoop out the centre of each slice, taking care not to pierce the base.

Preheat the oven to 220°C (425°F or Mark 7). Cook the courgettes in boiling water until they are bright green and almost tender — about 1 minute. Drain them well in a sieve, and arrange them on a baking sheet lined with non-stick parchment paper.

To prepare the soufflé filling, place the margarine, flour and milk in a small heavy-bottomed saucepan, and whisk until the ingredients are well blended. Place the pan over medium heat and bring to the boil, whisking continuously. Reduce the heat and cook gently for 5 minutes, still whisking continuously. Remove the pan from the heat and whisk in the egg yolk, cheese, mustard, salt and some pepper, until evenly mixed.

In a clean bowl, whisk the egg whites until they are stiff but not dry. Add the egg white to the cheese sauce, one third at a time, carefully folding it into the mixture until all the egg white has been incorporated. Place teaspoons of the soufflé mixture into the courgette containers, filling each to the top.

Bake the soufflés at the top of the oven until the soufflé mixture has risen well and is golden-brown — 5 to 8 minutes. Arrange the courgette soufflés on a serving plate, and serve hot or warm.

EDITOR'S NOTE: *Variants of this recipe can be made with artichoke bottoms or hearts, mushrooms or tomato halves in place of the courgette slices.*

Feta and Phyllo Parcels

Makes 12 parcels
Working time: about 30 minutes
Total time: about 45 minutes

Per parcel:
Calories **75**
Protein **2g**
Cholesterol **5mg**
Total fat **6g**
Saturated fat **1g**
Sodium **130mg**

4	sheets phyllo pastry, each about 45 by 30 cm (18 by 12 inches)	4
3 tbsp	virgin olive oil	3 tbsp
125 g	feta cheese, rinsed, patted dry and cut into 12 pieces	4 oz
1 tbsp	finely chopped fresh mint	1 tbsp

Preheat the oven to 180°C (350°F or Mark 4).

Place one sheet of phyllo pastry on the worktop and brush a little of the olive oil on its upper surface. Then place a second phyllo sheet on top of the first and brush its upper surface with oil. Turn the two sheets over together and brush the upper surface. (Mean-while, keep the other two sheets of the phyllo pastry covered with a damp cloth to prevent them from drying out and becoming brittle.)

Using a saucer about 15 cm (6 inches) in diameter as a template, cut out six discs from the double sheet of oiled phyllo. Place a piece of feta cheese and a little chopped fresh mint in the centre of each disc. Gather up the phyllo edges carefully and twist them slightly to make a frill resembling a toffee wrapper. Transfer the phyllo parcels to a baking tin. Repeat with the remaining two phyllo sheets.

Bake the phyllo parcels on the lower shelf of the oven for 5 minutes, then reduce the oven temperature to 170°C (325°F or Mark 3) and bake the parcels until the bottoms and sides are evenly coloured — a further 10 to 15 minutes. Transfer them to a warm serving platter and serve at once.

Fir Apple Potato Canapés

FIR APPLE POTATOES ARE A VARIETY OF SMALL, ELONGATED WAXY POTATO. IF UNAVAILABLE, WAXY NEW POTATOES MAY BE USED INSTEAD.

Makes about 30 canapés
Working time: about 20 minutes
Total time: about 30 minutes

Per canapé:
Calories **25**
Protein **1g**
Cholesterol **5mg**
Total fat **1g**
Saturated fat **trace**
Sodium **30mg**

4	fir apple potatoes (about 350 g/12 oz), scrubbed and dried	4
30 g	unsalted butter	1 oz
2	garlic cloves, crushed	2
1 tbsp	finely chopped celery leaves	1 tbsp
1 tbsp	finely chopped parsley	1 tbsp
½ tsp	salt	½ tsp
	freshly ground black pepper	
4	orange segments, cut into slices, for garnish	4
Celery topping		
2	sticks celery, finely chopped	2
125 g	turkey breast fillet, chopped	4 oz
1 tbsp	pine-nuts, chopped	1 tbsp
1 tsp	finely grated orange rind	1 tsp
1 tsp	Dijon mustard	1 tsp

Preheat the oven to 220°C (425°F or Mark 7). Cut the potatoes into 5 mm (¼ inch) slices and cook them in a saucepan of boiling water for 1 minute, until they are almost tender. Drain the potato slices well and transfer them to a bowl.

Put the butter, crushed garlic, chopped celery leaves, parsley, salt and a little freshly ground pepper in the saucepan and stir until the butter has melted. Pour half of this mixture on to the potato slices in the bowl and toss well to coat them evenly.

Line a baking sheet with non-stick parchment paper. Remove the potatoes from the bowl with a slotted spoon, and arrange them, evenly spaced, on the baking sheet. Bake the slices in the oven until lightly browned — 4 to 5 minutes.

While the potatoes are baking, prepare the topping. Add the chopped celery, turkey fillet, pine-nuts, orange rind and mustard to the remaining garlic butter in the saucepan. Cook the mixture over moderate heat for 1 minute, stirring occasionally. Season with a little more pepper if desired.

Place spoonfuls of the mixture on top of each potato slice, dividing the mixture evenly. Return the potato slices to the top shelf of the oven and bake until the topping has set — about 5 minutes. Arrange the potato canapés on a serving plate and garnish each with a slice of orange. Serve hot or warm.

EDITOR'S NOTE: *In place of the turkey, you may substitute chicken, veal or white fish.*

Curried Vegetable Pancakes with Coriander-Lime Yogurt

Makes about 30 pancakes
Working (and total) time: about 1 hour

Per pancake:
Calories **25**
Protein **10g**
Cholesterol **1mg**
Total fat **1g**
Saturated fat **trace**
Sodium **40mg**

60 g	plain flour	2 oz
60 g	wholemeal flour	2 oz
½ tsp	baking powder	½ tsp
½ tsp	salt	½ tsp
1 tsp	punch puran	1 tsp
1 tsp	garam masala	1 tsp
1 tsp	ground turmeric	1 tsp
½ tsp	ground cardamom	½ tsp
12.5cl	plain low-fat yogurt	4 fl oz
1 tbsp	grapeseed or safflower oil	1 tbsp
100 g	sweet potato, peeled and finely diced or grated	3½ oz
100 g	celeriac, peeled and finely diced or grated	3½ oz
	Coriander-lime yogurt topping	
175 g	thick Greek yogurt	6 oz
⅛ tsp	salt	⅛ tsp
1 tsp	lime pickle	1 tsp
½ tsp	freshly grated lime rind	½ tsp
1	small bunch fresh coriander, chopped	1

Mix together all the ingredient for the coriander-lime yogurt topping. Pour into a serving bowl and chill in the refrigerator until ready to use.

To make the batter, first sift the flours, baking powder and salt into a mixing bowl. Dry-fry the punch puran in a fairly hot, heavy frying pan until the mixture smells highly aromatic — about 2 minutes. Add it to the flour with the garam masala, turmeric and cardamom, stir, and make a hollow in the centre of the flour. Mix the yogurt with 12.5 cl (4 fl oz) of water and pour into the well together with the oil. Blend, gradually incorporating the dry ingredients into the liquid. Beat lightly but thoroughly until no lumps remain. Stir in the sweet potato and celeriac.

Set a large griddle or heavy frying pan *(box, page 86)* over medium heat until a few drops of cold water dance when sprinkled on the surface. Drop tablespoons of the batter on to the griddle and use the back of the spoon to spread it into rounds. Cook the pancakes gently, a few at a time, over medium heat for 4 to 5 minutes on each side, until lightly browned — cut one through to test the tenderness of the vegetables. Transfer to a platter, cover loosely with foil and keep warm in a 170°C (325°F or Mark 3) oven while you cook the remaining batter. (If the pancakes stick, wipe the pan lightly with oil before each batch.)

Serve the warm pancakes topped with a teaspoon of the coriander-lime yogurt.

SUGGESTED ACCOMPANIMENT: *lime pickle.*

EDITOR'S NOTE: Punch puran, a mixture of cumin, fennel seed, mustard seed, onion seed and fenugreek, is obtainable from Asian shops — as are garam masala, turmeric and cardamom.

Tricolour Tortellini Filled with Mushrooms

Makes about 60 tortellini
Working (and total) time: about 3 hours

Per 3 tortellini:
Calories **180**
Protein **8g**
Cholesterol **15mg**
Total fat **5g**
Saturated fat **1g**
Sodium **95mg**

⅛ tsp	saffron strands	⅛ tsp
½ tsp	salt	½ tsp
350 g	strong plain flour	12 oz
125 g	fine semolina	4 oz
2	small eggs, beaten	2
2 tbsp	tomato paste	2 tbsp
60 g	cooked spinach, drained thoroughly, finely chopped	2 oz
1 tbsp	virgin olive oil	1 tbsp
Mushroom filling		
1 tsp	virgin olive oil	1 tsp
2	garlic cloves, crushed	2
60 g	dried ceps, soaked for about 20 minutes in 15 cl (¼ pint) hot water	2 oz
350 g	large flat mushrooms, wiped clean and finely chopped	12 oz
2	fresh thyme sprigs, leaves only	2
¼ tsp	salt	¼ tsp
1 tbsp	Marsala or brandy	1 tbsp
¼ tsp	grated nutmeg	¼ tsp
¼ tsp	freshly ground black pepper	¼ tsp
75 g	low-fat ricotta cheese	2½ oz
2 tbsp	parsley, finely chopped	2 tbsp
Soft cheese dip (optional)		
3	garlic cloves, crushed	3
1 tsp	virgin olive oil	1 tsp
400 g	fromage frais	14 oz
4 tbsp	parsley, finely chopped	4 tbsp
½ tsp	finely grated lemon rind	½ tsp
¼ tsp	salt	¼ tsp

To make the cheese dip, sauté the crushed garlic in the oil for 5 minutes, then transfer the garlic to a bowl. Add the *fromage frais*, parsley, lemon rind and salt, and blend the mixture with a fork; set aside.

To prepare the filling, put the oil and garlic in a small saucepan, cover and place over a low heat for 5 minutes. Meanwhile, remove the dried mushrooms from their soaking liquid, rinse them thoroughly and chop them finely; filter the soaking liquid through a coffee filter paper and reserve 3 tablespoons. In a wide, heavy sauté pan, combine the soaked dried mushrooms with the fresh mushrooms, garlic, thyme, salt, reserved soaking liquid and Marsala or brandy. Cover the pan and simmer the mixture over low heat for 20 minutes. Then remove the lid, increase the heat, and cook briskly for a few seconds to eliminate excess moisture, stirring continuously. Transfer the mixture to a bowl, season with the nutmeg and pepper, and beat in the ricotta and the parsley with a wooden spoon. Set aside to cool while you make the three pastas.

Grind the saffron strands with a little of the salt in a mortar and pestle. Put one third of the flour, one third of the semolina, one third of the beaten egg and the saffron in the bowl of a food processor. Using the metal chopping blade, process for about 30 seconds until fine crumbs are formed. Add water — up to 4 tablespoons — a little at a time, through the feeder-funnel until the dough forms a single large ball. Place it in a bowl, cover with plastic film and set aside.

In the processor, combine half the remaining flour, semolina, salt and beaten egg to form fine crumbs. Add the tomato paste, and process until small lumps are formed. After a few seconds, add water, a little at a time, until the dough forms a ball. Put the dough in a bowl, cover it and set it aside.

Combine the remaining flour, semolina, salt and egg

Shaping Tortellini

1 ADDING THE FILLING. With a 5 cm (2 inch) biscuit cutter, stamp circles from a sheet of pasta dough. In the middle of each circle, put a ½ teaspoon of filling. Using a pastry brush or your finger, moisten the edge of the circle with water (above).

2 MAKING THE FIRST FOLD. Fold over the circle of dough to form a half-moon containing the filling. To seal in the filling, pinch the moistened edges of the dough together between your thumb and forefinger (above).

3 BENDING INTO SHAPE. Take one end of each half-moon in either hand and curve it gently until its ends are just overlapping. At the same time, fold the sealed margin of the dough back towards the straight edge of the shape, to make a groove round the edge (above). Pinch the ends firmly together, so that the shape remains curled round.

as above. Add the spinach and process until small lumps are formed. Continue processing, adding water a little at a time if necessary, until the dough forms a ball. Transfer it to a bowl, cover and set aside.

Divide the ball of saffron dough into quarters and pass one quarter at a time through successive settings of a manual pasta extruder, stopping at the penultimate setting; flour the dough whenever it feels sticky. Cover three of the sheets of dough with a damp cloth to prevent them from drying out. Using a 5 cm (2 inch) round biscuit cutter, cut as many circles as possible from the remaining pasta sheet. Fill and shape the saffron circles into tortellini *(left)* and discard the trimmings. Repeat with the remaining sheets of saffron dough. Put the completed tortellini on a floured surface; ensure that they are not touching. Quarter and roll out the other two pasta balls and assemble tomato and spinach tortellini in the same way.

In a large saucepan, bring 2 litres (3½ pints) of lightly salted water to the boil. Gently drop about a quarter of the tortellini into the water, bring back to the boil and cook for 3 to 5 minutes until they rise to the surface. Remove from the water with a slotted spoon, drain well and brush lightly with the oil. Cook the remainder in batches in the same way, keeping the cooked tortellini warm in a covered container in a low oven. Thread the tortellini on to skewers or offer them with cocktail sticks. Serve hot, with the dip if you wish.

EDITOR'S NOTE: *The pasta dough can be made and rolled out by hand: add the beaten egg, flavourings and 2 to 3 tablespoons of water to the flour mixture, and knead it for about 5 minutes, adding more water if necessary until the dough has formed into smooth, elastic balls. Rest the dough, covered, for about 1 hour. When rolling out the dough, keep the surfaces floured so that the pasta does not stick, and roll as quickly as you can; press quite hard and roll the pasta as thinly as possible.*

Baby Potatoes Coated with Herbs and Parmesan

Makes about 30 potatoes
Working (and total) time: about 20 minutes

Per potato:
Calories **65**
Protein **2g**
Cholesterol **trace**
Total fat **3g**
Saturated fat **1g**
Sodium **60mg**

1.5 kg	small new potatoes, scrubbed	3 lb
4 tbsp	virgin olive oil	4 tbsp
60 g	Parmesan cheese, freshly grated	2 oz
30 g	fresh dill, chives, parsley or mint, or any combination of these, chopped	1 oz
½ tsp	salt	½ tsp
	freshly ground black pepper	

Boil the potatoes until they are just soft — about 15 minutes — then drain them thoroughly.

Place the oil, cheese, herbs and salt in a large bowl with a generous grinding of pepper. Add the potatoes and toss them until they are well coated with the mixture. Serve hot or warm, speared with cocktail sticks.

Anchovy-Tomato Dip

Serves 10
Working (and total) time: about 1 hour

Calories **55**
Protein **3g**
Cholesterol **trace**
Total fat **2g**
Saturated fat **trace**
Sodium **155mg**

7	garlic cloves	7
1 tbsp	virgin olive oil	1 tbsp
4	anchovy fillets, rinsed and drained	4
750 g	plum tomatoes, skinned, seeded (page 76) and coarsely chopped	1½ lb
¾ tsp	powdered dried oregano	¾ tsp
1½ tbsp	tomato paste	1½ tbsp
1½ tbsp	red wine vinegar	1½ tbsp
1½ tsp	molasses or other dark brown sugar	1½ tsp
250 g	broccoli florets	8 oz
175 g	mushrooms	6 oz
1 tbsp	chopped fresh basil	1 tbsp
1	sweet red pepper, seeded, deribbed and cut into 2.5 cm (1 inch) squares	1
1	sweet yellow pepper, seeded, deribbed and cut into 2.5 cm (1 inch) squares	1
350 g	cauliflower florets	12 oz

Put the garlic and oil in a heavy-bottomed saucepan and cook over low heat, crushing the garlic cloves with a wooden spoon as they soften. After about 10 minutes, add the anchovies to the pan and cook for a further 5 minutes, stirring constantly and crushing the anchovies; do not allow the mixture to burn. Add the tomatoes, oregano, tomato paste, vinegar and sugar, and simmer for 20 to 30 minutes, stirring occasionally.

Meanwhile, pour enough water into a saucepan to fill it 2.5 cm (1 inch) deep. Set a steamer in the pan and bring the water to the boil. Put the broccoli in the steamer, cover the pan tightly, and steam for just 1 minute. Remove from the steamer and set aside. Wipe the mushrooms with a clean, damp cloth, cut into bite-sized pieces and set aside.

Sieve the tomato sauce over a bowl, pressing firmly with a spoon to push through as much pulp as possible. Stir in the basil. Transfer the sauce to a small fondue pot and set over a gentle flame.

Arrange the broccoli, mushrooms, peppers and cauliflower on a serving platter and provide fondue forks or long bamboo sticks for spearing the morsels and dipping them into the hot sauce.

EDITOR'S NOTE: *The sauce may be prepared in advance and gently reheated just before serving; add the chopped fresh basil at the last minute.*

Stuffed Courgettes and Baby Onions

Makes 48 pieces
Working (and total) time: about 1 hour and 10 minutes

Per piece:
Calories **15**
Protein **trace**
Cholesterol **0mg**
Total fat **1g**
Saturated fat **trace**
Sodium **25mg**

12	pearl onions	12
2 tbsp	virgin olive oil	2 tbsp
3	garlic cloves, crushed	3
500 g	ripe tomatoes, skinned, seeded (page 76) and chopped	1 lb
1 tbsp	finely cut fresh basil leaves, or 1 tsp dried basil	1 tbsp
2 tsp	tomato paste	2 tsp
½ tsp	salt	½ tsp
	freshly ground black pepper	
3	courgettes, each about 15 cm (6 inches) long	3
1 tbsp	sugar	1 tbsp
30 g	fresh wholemeal breadcrumbs	1 oz
1 tsp	dried mixed herbs	1 tsp
15 g	Parmesan cheese, finely grated	½ oz

Skin the onions and trim the bottoms so that they will stand level. Cut about 5 mm (¼ inch) off the top of each onion, then very carefully scoop out the centre with a grapefruit spoon or sharp knife to leave a hollow case — the walls should be about 5 mm (¼ inch) thick. Set the onions aside.

Finely chop the onion trimmings and centres. Heat 1 tablespoon of the oil in a heavy-bottomed saucepan, add the chopped onion and cook very gently until softened, but not browned — 4 to 5 minutes. Stir in the garlic, tomatoes and basil. Partially cover the saucepan and cook until the tomatoes are soft and well reduced to form a thick mixture. Stir in the tomato paste and season with a little of the salt and some pepper. Pour the tomato mixture into a nylon sieve placed over a bowl, and allow excess liquid to drain off while you prepare the courgettes and onions.

Trim the courgettes and cut them in half lengthwise. Season the onions and courgettes with the remaining salt and a little black pepper.

Heat the remaining oil in a wide, shallow sauté pan or heavy frying pan with a lid. Add the sugar and heat gently until it dissolves and turns a golden caramel colour. Reduce the heat to low, add the onions and turn them in the caramel until they are lightly browned all over. Move the onions to one side of the pan and add the courgettes, placing them cut side down. Cover the pan and cook the vegetables for 5 to 8 minutes, until they are tender but still firm.

Preheat the grill to high. Fill each onion with a little of the tomato mixture, then spoon the rest neatly down the centre of the courgettes. Cut each courgette half into six equal pieces.

Place the vegetables in the grill pan. Mix together the wholemeal breadcrumbs, dried mixed herbs and grated Parmesan cheese, and sprinkle the mixture over the stuffed vegetables. Cook under the grill until golden-brown. Serve warm.

EDITOR'S NOTE: *The vegetables may be prepared and filled ahead of time, leaving only the grilling to be done when you are ready to serve them.*

Folding Phyllo Packages

1 MAKING THE FIRST FOLD. Position a strip of phyllo with a short side towards you. Brush the strip lightly with butter. Place a teaspoon of filling on the phyllo about 2 cm (¾ inch) from the end nearest you. Lift one corner of the strip and fold it over the filling so that the corner meets the opposite long side, creating a triangle.

2 MAKING THE SECOND FOLD. Using both hands, lift the triangle of phyllo containing the filling and fold it away from you.

3 COMPLETING THE PACKAGE. Continue folding the package alternately across and up the strip until you reach the far end; any short band of phyllo remaining at the far end may be trimmed off or folded round the package.

Miniature Samosas

Makes 32 samosas
Working (and total) time: about 1 hour and 15 minutes

			Per samosa:
250 g	potatoes, peeled and chopped	8oz	Calories **25**
90 g	carrots, sliced	3oz	Protein **1g**
7 g	dried ceps, soaked for 20 minutes in hot water	¼ oz	Cholesterol **3mg** Total fat **1g**
1 tsp	poppy seeds	1 tsp	Saturated fat **1g**
40 g	unsalted butter	1¼ oz	Sodium **35mg**
1	small onion, finely chopped	1	
60 g	shelled young fresh or frozen peas	2 oz	
1 cm	piece fresh ginger root, finely chopped	½ inch	
½ tsp	garam masala	½ tsp	
½ tsp	salt	½ tsp	
⅛ tsp	cayenne pepper	⅛ tsp	
4	sheets phyllo pastry, each about 45 by 30 cm (18 by 12 inches)	4	
	coriander sprigs, for garnish		
	Coriander-yogurt dip		
15	coriander sprigs, leaves only, finely chopped	15	
¼ litre	plain low-fat yogurt	8 fl oz	
	freshly ground black pepper		

Boil the potatoes and carrots separately until they are tender — 12 to 15 minutes. Drain and leave to cool. Chop the carrots into small dice and coarsely mash the potatoes. Drain and squeeze dry the ceps, and chop them finely.

Toast the poppy seeds in a dry frying pan until they start to change colour, then remove from the heat.

Melt 7 g (¼ oz) of the butter in a heavy frying pan over medium heat and fry the onion until golden-brown. Add the peas, mushrooms and ginger, and cook for 2 to 3 minutes, stirring continuously. Add the potatoes and carrots, and mix well. Remove from the heat, stir in the garam masala, salt and cayenne pepper, and set the filling aside.

Preheat the oven to 200°C (400°F or Mark 6). Cut one sheet of phyllo into eight strips measuring about 30 by 5.5 cm (12 by 2¼ inches). Keep the phyllo you are not working on covered with a damp cloth. Melt the remaining butter and lightly brush one side of each phyllo strip, then make up the strips into triangular packages, each enclosing about 1 teaspoon of filling, as demonstrated opposite. Place the phyllo packages on a lightly greased or non-stick baking sheet with the loose ends underneath. Bake in the oven for 15 to 20 minutes, until golden-brown.

To make the dip, mix the coriander into the yogurt and season with some pepper. Serve the samosas hot, garnished with the coriander sprigs and accompanied by the coriander-yogurt dip.

Spinach and Ricotta Calzone

Makes 30 calzone
Working time: about 40 minutes
Total time: about 1 hour and 30 minutes

Per calzone:
Calories **85**
Protein **4g**
Cholesterol **10mg**
Total fat **2g**
Saturated fat **1g**
Sodium **150mg**

½ tsp	sugar	½ tsp
30 g	fresh yeast, or 15 g (½ oz) dried yeast	1 oz
500 g	strong plain flour	1 lb
1 tsp	salt	1 tsp
1 tbsp	virgin olive oil	1 tbsp
1	egg yolk beaten with 2 tsp water	1
Spinach and ricotta filling		
500 g	spinach, washed, stems removed	1 lb
125 g	low-fat ricotta cheese	4 oz
½ tsp	grated nutmeg	½ tsp
1 tsp	pesto	1 tsp
¼ tsp	salt	¼ tsp
	freshly ground black pepper	
125 g	low-fat mozzarella, finely cubed	4 oz

To make the dough for the calzone, first stir the sugar into 30 cl (½ pint) of tepid water, then blend in the fresh yeast. Leave to activate until the mixture is frothy — 10 to 15 minutes. If you are using dried yeast, reconstitute according to the manufacturer's instructions. Sift the flour and salt into a large bowl and make a well in the centre. Pour in the yeast liquid and the olive oil and mix, gradually incorporating all the flour into the liquid. Remove the dough from the bowl and knead until it is silky to the touch — about 5 minutes. Add a little more flour if the dough is sticky. Put the dough into a lightly oiled bowl and leave in a warm place until the dough has risen to double its size — about 45 minutes.

While the dough is rising, make the filling. Place the spinach with water still clinging to the leaves in a large saucepan. Cover, and steam the spinach over medium heat until wilted — 2 to 3 minutes. Drain and squeeze out all water. Put the spinach into a blender or food processor with the ricotta, nutmeg, pesto, salt and some freshly ground pepper, and blend very briefly. Then stir in the mozzarella cubes.

Preheat the oven to 220°C (425°C or Mark 7).

When the dough has risen, place it on a work surface and knead it slightly to knock it down. Roll out the dough as thinly as possible and cut out 30 circles with a 7.5 cm (3 inch) pastry cutter. Put about a teaspoon of the filling in the centre of each circle, moisten the circumference with a little of the egg yolk and water, then fold over and seal in a semi-circle. Brush the tops of each calzone with the remaining egg yolk and water, then make a small incision in each one.

Bake the calzone until well risen and golden in colour — 8 to 10 minutes. Serve warm.

EDITOR'S NOTE: *The dough may be prepared in advance and refrigerated for up to 24 hours.*

Aubergine, Tomato and Crab Croustades

Makes 12 croustades
Working time: about 30 minutes
Total time: about 35 minutes

Per croustade:
Calories **90**
Protein **4g**
Cholesterol **10mg**
Total fat **4g**
Saturated fat **1g**
Sodium **80mg**

12	thin slices white bread	12
3 tbsp	virgin olive oil	3 tbsp
250 g	aubergine, peeled and roughly chopped	8 oz
1	garlic clove finely chopped	1
125 g	tomatoes, skinned, seeded (page 76) and roughly chopped	4 oz
½	lemon, juice only	½
½ tsp	salt	½ tsp
	freshly ground black pepper	
125 g	white crab meat, picked over	4 oz
	lemon slices, for garnish	

Preheat the oven to 200°C (400°F or Mark 6).

Using a 7.5 cm (3 inch) diameter round pastry cutter, cut out a circle from each slice of bread. Brush both sides of the bread circles lightly with 2 tablespoons of the oil and press them firmly into 12 tartlet tins. Cook in the oven until the bread is golden-brown and has set into shape — about 10 minutes.

Meanwhile, prepare the filling. Heat the remaining oil in a heavy frying pan over medium heat and sauté the aubergine with the garlic. When the aubergine is well browned, stir in the tomato, lemon juice, salt and some pepper. Increase the heat to evaporate all the juices, then spoon the mixture into the croustade cases. Flake the crab meat and distribute it among the cases.

Cover the croustades loosely with aluminium foil or a sheet of greaseproof paper and return the tray to the hot oven for 5 minutes. Serve hot, garnished with the slices of lemon.

Pissaladière Tartlets

Makes 24 tartlets
Working time: about 1 hour
Total time: about 1 hour and 45 minutes

Per tartlet:
Calories **70**
Protein **2g**
Cholesterol **trace**
Total fat **3g**
Saturated fat **trace**
Sodium **45mg**

1 ½ tbsp	virgin olive oil	1 ½ tbsp
2	large onions (about 750 g/1 ½ lb), quartered and thinly sliced	2
1	large garlic clove, finely chopped	1
6	anchovy fillets, soaked in milk for 30 minutes, rinsed in cold water and patted dry	6
12	black olives, stoned and quartered	12
Tartlet dough		
15 g	fresh yeast, or 7 g (¼ oz) dried yeast	½ oz
250 g	strong plain flour	8 oz
¼ tsp	salt	¼ tsp
1 ½ tbsp	virgin olive oil	1 ½ tbsp
1 tsp	chopped fresh rosemary, or ½ tsp dried rosemary	1 tsp

First prepare the dough. Dissolve the fresh yeast in 2 tablespoons of tepid water; if using dried yeast, reconstitute according to the manufacturer's instructions. Sift the flour and salt into a large bowl, make a well in the centre and pour in the yeast solution. Add 1 tablespoon of the oil, the rosemary and 12.5 cl (4 fl oz)

of tepid water, and mix to make a soft but not sticky dough. On a floured work surface, knead the dough until it is smooth and elastic — about 5 minutes.

Put the remaining ½ tablespoon of oil in a mixing bowl. Form the dough into a ball and put it into the bowl; turn the dough to coat it all over with oil. Cover the bowl with a damp tea towel and leave the dough in a warm place to rise, until it has doubled in size — about 1 hour.

While the dough rises, prepare the filling. Heat the oil in a large frying pan and sauté the onion and garlic for 40 minutes over low heat, adding a little water if necessary to prevent them from sticking.

Cut each anchovy fillet lengthwise into four strips, then halve the strips by cutting across them.

Preheat the oven to 200°C (400°F or Mark 6). Knock back the dough, then turn it out on to a lightly floured surface and knead briefly. Cut the dough into 24 portions. Roll out each portion into a circle about 6 cm (2½ inches) in diameter, and use the circles to line 6 cm (2½ inch) diameter tartlet tins.

Fill each dough case with a heaped teaspoon of the onion mixture and smooth the surface. Cross two anchovy strips on each tartlet, and add two olive quarters. Place the tartlet tins on a baking sheet and bake until the dough has risen and is lightly golden — about 15 minutes. Serve hot.

Aubergine Sausages

Makes about 40 sausages
Working time: about 1 hour
Total time: about 1 hour and 30 minutes (includes soaking)

Per sausage:
Calories **35**
Protein **2g**
Cholesterol **5mg**
Total fat **2g**
Saturated fat **1g**
Sodium **65mg**

750 g	aubergines	1 ½ lb
250 g	potatoes, peeled and chopped	8 oz
175 g	fresh brown breadcrumbs	6 oz
125 g	low-fat soft cheese	4 oz
1	egg, lightly beaten	1
2	shallots, finely chopped	2
2 tsp	tomato paste	2 tsp
1 tbsp	chopped parsley	1 tbsp
1 tbsp	chopped fresh rosemary	1 tbsp
1 tsp	grated nutmeg	1 tsp
½ tsp	salt	½ tsp
	freshly ground black pepper	
2 metres	natural lamb sausage casing, soaked in acidulated water for 1 hour	6 feet
1 tsp	safflower oil	1 tsp
2 tsp	clear honey	2 tsp
	Green peppercorn dip	
250 g	fromage frais	8 oz
2 tsp	green peppercorns	2 tsp
2 tbsp	chopped capers	2 tbsp
1 tbsp	chopped fresh tarragon	1 tbsp
2 tsp	tarragon vinegar	2 tsp

Preheat the oven to 220°C (425°F or Mark 7). Cut the aubergines in half lengthwise and place them cut side down on a foil-lined baking sheet. Bake them until they are tender — 20 to 30 minutes.

Meanwhile, cook the potatoes in boiling water until they are almost tender — 3 to 5 minutes. Drain them and set aside.

Remove the cooked aubergines from the oven, but leave the oven on. Scoop the flesh out of the aubergines and discard the skins. In a food processor, purée the aubergine flesh, potatoes, breadcrumbs and soft cheese. Add the egg, shallots, tomato paste, parsley, rosemary, nutmeg, salt and some pepper, and process until the mixture is thoroughly blended.

Unravel the sausage casings and cut them in two. Roll one end of a length of casing over the spout of a funnel or tap and run cold water through it to open it out, then rinse the other length in the same way. Drain the casings. Make up the 2.5 cm (1 inch) sausages as demonstrated on page 98.

Place the linked sausages on a lightly greased baking sheet and brush them with the oil. Bake in the oven for 12 to 15 minutes, until golden-brown.

Meanwhile, mix together the ingredients for the peppercorn dip and pour into a serving bowl. Then warm the honey in a small saucepan over low heat.

Allow the cooked sausages to cool for 2 to 3 minutes before cutting through the links with kitchen scissors. Brush the sausages with the warmed honey and arrange them on a serving dish. Serve hot with the green peppercorn dip.

EDITOR'S NOTE: *Natural sausage casings — the cleansed intestines of lamb, pig or ox — can be ordered from your butcher or from specialist suppliers. Use lamb casings for small sausages, as shown here.*

Sigara Borek with Asparagus and Parmesan

BOREK IS A TURKISH WORD FOR A PASTRY-WRAPPED SAVOURY; SIGARA IS A CIGARETTE.

Makes 12 *sigara*
Working time: about 15 minutes
Total time: about 30 minutes

Per sigara:
Calories **20**
Protein **1g**
Cholesterol **trace**
Total fat **1g**
Saturated fat **trace**
Sodium **15mg**

12	asparagus spears, trimmed and peeled	12
2	sheets phyllo pastry, each about 45 by 30 cm (18 by 12 inches)	2
3 tsp	freshly grated Parmesan cheese	3 tsp
	freshly ground black pepper	
½ tbsp	virgin olive oil	½ tbsp

Trim the asparagus spears to about 10 cm (4 inches) long, discarding any excess stalk. Cook the spears in boiling water for 3 minutes, then drain them in a colander and refresh under cold running water. Drain the spears well and pat them dry with paper towels.

Preheat the oven to 200°C (400°F or Mark 6).

Lay out the sheets of phyllo pastry on a lightly floured board. Cut each in half lengthwise, then across three times to make 12 squares about 15 by 15 cm (6 by 6 inches). Sprinkle the phyllo squares evenly with the Parmesan cheese.

Keeping the phyllo you are not working on covered with a damp cloth to prevent it from drying out, lay an asparagus spear on a phyllo square, about 2.5 cm (1 inch) in from one edge, and sprinkle with a little black pepper. Fold the edge over the asparagus, then fold in the two adjacent sides at a slight angle, so that the side of the square opposite the spear is narrower. Roll up the spear into a neat cigarette shape and brush each one with a little of the oil. Make the remaining asparagus rolls in the same way.

Bake the *sigara* in the oven for 10 to 15 minutes, turning once so that they brown evenly. Serve hot.

Butterflying a Prawn

1 *CUTTING THE UNDERSHELL. Remove and discard the head of the prawn and gently pull off the legs. Using small kitchen scissors, cut the undershell of the prawn along its length.*

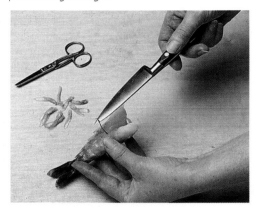

2 *SLITTING THE PRAWN. Using a sharp knife, slit open the prawn; cut right through the prawn to its shell without splitting the shell. Remove the intestinal tract running down the back of the prawn and discard.*

3 *OPENING OUT THE PRAWN. Lay the prawn on the work surface, cut side down. Press hard with your fingers along the spine of the shell until it cracks. Alternatively, slit the prawn and shell lengthwise, leaving 1 cm (½ inch) intact in the centre of the spine, and push the cut ends apart for a full butterfly effect.*

Ginger-Spiced Prawns

Makes 12 prawns
Working time: about 30 minutes
Total time: about 2 hours and 30 minutes
(includes marinating)

Per prawn:
Calories **30**
Protein **3g**
Cholesterol **20mg**
Total fat **2g**
Saturated fat **trace**
Sodium **30mg**

12	raw Mediterranean prawns (about 500 g/1 lb), gutted and butterflied (left)	12
4 tbsp	low-sodium soy sauce or shoyu	4 tbsp
2 tsp	fresh lemon or lime juice	2 tsp
2 tsp	honey	2 tsp
2.5 cm	piece fresh ginger root, peeled and finely chopped, or the juice extracted with a garlic press	1 inch
1	garlic clove, finely chopped	1
½ tsp	Chinese five-spice powder	½ tsp
1 tbsp	light sesame oil	1 tbsp
	lettuce leaves, washed, dried and shredded, for garnish	
	lemon wedges, for garnish (optional)	

Combine the soy sauce, lemon or lime juice, honey, ginger, garlic and five-spice powder in a wide, shallow, non-reactive dish. Place the butterflied prawns in this mixture, flesh side down, and leave to marinate in a cool place for 2 hours.

Preheat the grill to high, and brush a wide, fireproof pan with 1 teaspoon of the oil. Reserving the marinade, place the prawns, flesh side down, in the pan. Brush the shells of the prawns with the remaining oil and grill for 3 to 5 minutes, turning once, until the shells turn pink and the flesh is no longer translucent.

Meanwhile, reduce the reserved marinade in a small saucepan over high heat until only 1 tablespoon remains. Brush this glaze over both sides of the prawns. Serve immediately on a bed of the shredded lettuce, accompanied, if you like, with lemon wedges.

Mussels on the Half Shell

Makes 20 mussels
Working (and total) time: 30 minutes

Per mussel: Calories **25** Protein **4g** Cholesterol **10mg** Total fat **1g** Saturated fat **trace** Sodium **70mg**	20	mussels (about 500 g/1 lb), scrubbed and debearded	20
	1	lemon, cut into wedges	1
	Tomato and fennel relish		
	2 tsp	virgin olive oil	2 tsp
	60 g	bulb fennel, finely chopped	2 oz
	250 g	tomatoes, skinned, seeded (page 76) and chopped	8 oz
	½ tsp	sherry vinegar	½ tsp
	1 tsp	tomato paste	1 tsp
	1	garlic clove, crushed	1
	¼ tsp	salt	¼ tsp
		freshly ground black pepper	
	15 g	wild fennel or parsley, finely chopped	½ oz

Pour 4 tablespoons of water into a large pan. Add the mussels, cover the pan and bring the water to the boil. Steam the mussels until their shells open — 4 to 5 minutes. Discard any mussels that remain closed.

Remove the top shell from each of the mussels and discard. Using your fingers or a spoon, sever the connective tissue that attaches the mussel to the bottom shell. Return the mussels to their half shells and place them in an ovenproof serving dish. Preheat the oven to 190°C (375°F or Mark 5).

To make the tomato and fennel relish, first pour the oil into a heavy-bottomed saucepan over medium heat and sauté the fennel until fairly soft — about 5 minutes. Add the tomatoes, vinegar, tomato paste, garlic, salt and some pepper, and simmer until the mixture is well reduced — about 10 minutes. Stir in the wild fennel or parsley.

Spoon a little of the relish on to each half mussel shell. Cover the dish with aluminium foil and put it in the oven for about 5 minutes, long enough for the mussels and relish to warm through. Serve immediately with the lemon wedges.

Skinning and Seeding a Tomato

1 *SKINNING THE TOMATO. Core the tomato by cutting a conical plug from its stem end. Cut a shallow cross in the base. Immerse the tomato in boiling water for 10 to 30 seconds, then plunge it into cold water. When the tomato has cooled, peel the skin away from the cross in sections.*

2 *SEEDING THE TOMATO. Halve the skinned tomato. Gently squeeze one of the halves, forcing out its seeds and juice. Rotate the tomato 90 degrees and squeeze once more. Dislodge any seeds from the inner chambers. Repeat the process with the other half.*

Red-Hot Monkfish

Makes about 50 bite-sized pieces
Working time: about 25 minutes
Total time: about 1 hour and 10 minutes

Per piece:	1.25 kg	ripe tomatoes, roughly chopped, or 800 g/28 oz canned tomatoes, drained	2½ lb
Calories **25**	2½ tbsp	virgin olive oil	2½ tbsp
Protein **3g**	1	small onion, finely chopped	1
Cholesterol **10mg**	2	garlic cloves, crushed	2
Total fat **1g**	1	small sweet green pepper, seeded, deribbed and finely chopped	1
Saturated fat **trace**			
Sodium **20mg**	15 g	fresh green chili pepper, seeded and finely chopped (caution, page 18)	½ oz
	⅛ tsp	chili powder	⅛ tsp
	1 tsp	caster sugar	1 tsp
	1 tsp	Dijon mustard	1 tsp
	1 tsp	fresh lemon juice	1 tsp
	¼ tsp	salt	¼ tsp
		freshly ground black pepper	
	1 kg	filleted and skinned monkfish	2¼ lb

Tip the tomatoes into a nylon sieve set over a bowl, and push them through the sieve with a wooden spoon to make a thin purée. Discard the pips and solids that collect in the sieve. Set the purée aside.

Heat ½ tablespoon of the oil in a heavy-bottomed saucepan and gently sweat the onion until soft but not coloured. Add the garlic and sweet green pepper, stir for a minute or two, then add the chili, tomato purée, chili powder, sugar, mustard and lemon juice.

Bring to a vigorous boil then lower the heat and maintain a light boil until the sauce has reduced to about 35 cl (12 fl oz) — about 40 minutes. Add the salt and a little black pepper. Set aside.

Trim the monkfish of any loose membrane and cut it into about fifty 2.5 cm (1 inch) cubes. Heat 1 table-spoon of the remaining oil in a large sauté pan and cook half of the fish pieces for 2 to 3 minutes, until just done. Using a slotted spoon, transfer the fish to the sauce. Clean the pan, add the remaining oil and cook the remaining fish pieces in the same way. Transfer the fish to the sauce and heat through.

Pour a little sauce on to a warm serving dish. Arrange the monkfish pieces on top and then pour over any remaining sauce. Serve hot with cocktail sticks to spear the fish.

Scallop and Lime Choux Puffs

Makes 16 puffs
Working time: about 40 minutes
Total time: about 1 hour and 20 minutes

Per puff:
Calories **80**
Protein **6g**
Cholesterol **45mg**
Total fat **4g**
Saturated fat **2g**
Sodium **105mg**

350 g	raw scallops, bright white connective tissue removed, rinsed and cut into 5 mm (¼ inch) dice	12 oz
1 ½ tsp	cornflour	1 ½ tsp
1 ½ tbsp	fresh lime juice	1 ½ tbsp
¼ tsp	grated lime rind	¼ tsp
1 ½ tbsp	finely chopped parsley	1 ½ tbsp
¼ tsp	salt	¼ tsp
	freshly ground black pepper	
60 g	fromage frais	2 oz
Choux dough		
60 g	unsalted butter	2 oz
¼ tsp	salt	¼ tsp
75 g	plain flour	2 ½ oz
2	eggs	2
	cayenne pepper	

To make the choux dough, place the butter and salt in a small heavy-bottomed saucepan containing 15 cl (¼ pint) of water, and heat to boiling point. Add all the flour, and beat the mixture until it comes away cleanly from the pan sides. Remove the pan from the heat.

Beat the eggs with a little cayenne pepper, then add them to the dough; beat until the eggs are absorbed and a stiff, glossy paste is formed.

Preheat the oven to 230°C (450°F or Mark 8).

Lightly oil a baking sheet. Fit a piping bag with a 2 cm (¾ inch) plain nozzle, fill it with choux dough and pipe 16 walnut-sized rounds on to the baking sheet. Cook the choux rounds in the oven for 10 minutes, then reduce the heat to 180°C (350°F or Mark 4) and cook for a further 25 to 30 minutes until the puffs are well risen and golden.

Slice through each choux puff about a third of the way from the top to allow the steam to escape, and leave to cool on a wire rack until required.

For the filling, sprinkle the scallops with the cornflour, turning and mixing to coat them evenly. Heat a dry, non-stick pan over high heat, add the scallops and, stirring all the time, sear them until they begin to colour — about 1 minute. Reduce the heat, add the lime juice and rind, parsley, salt, some pepper and the *fromage frais* to the pan, and continue to cook, stirring, until the juices thicken — about 2 minutes.

Warm the choux puffs through in a 180°C (350°F or Mark 4) oven. Spoon the scallop filling into the puffs and serve immediately.

EDITOR'S NOTE: *The choux puffs may be prepared in advance and stored in an airtight container for up to five days before being warmed through and filled. Alternatively, they can be frozen, and thawed in the oven as they are needed.*

Two-Salmon Wontons

Makes 16 wontons
Working time: about 20 minutes
Total time: about 1 hour (includes marinating)

Per wonton:			
Calories **55**	175 g	fresh salmon steaks	6 oz
Protein **3g**	60 g	smoked salmon, finely chopped	2 oz
Cholesterol **10mg**	1 tbsp	fresh lemon juice	1 tbsp
Total fat **2g**	1 tsp	finely chopped fresh dill	1 tsp
Saturated fat **trace**		freshly ground black pepper	
Sodium **85mg**	16	wonton wrappers	16

Skin the fresh salmon and remove all bones; run your fingers over the flesh to find the smaller bones, and remove these with tweezers. Finely chop the flesh and mix it together with the smoked salmon, lemon juice, dill and some black pepper. Leave to marinate for 30 minutes to 1 hour.

Place about a teaspoon of the salmon mixture in the centre of each wonton wrapper. Dip your fingertips in water and moisten the edges of each wrapper, then bring the four corners together to meet in the centre and press the edges together.

Place the wontons in a bamboo or lightly oiled stainless-steel steamer, cover and steam over boiling water until the wrappers become translucent — 2 to 5 minutes. Serve immediately.

EDITOR'S NOTE: *If wonton wrappers are not available, you can make your own. Mix 1 egg with 4 tablespoons of water and knead with 250 g (8 oz) of sifted plain flour for 5 to 10 minutes. Divide the dough in half and roll out each half thinly into a 35 cm (14 inch) square. Trim the edges and cut each square into 16 equal pieces. The wrappers not used for this recipe may be kept in the refrigerator for up to two days, or frozen.*

Sesame-Prawn Toasts

Makes 48 toasts
Working time: about 45 minutes
Total time: about 1 hour

Per toast:
Calories **15**
Protein **1g**
Cholesterol **5mg**
Total fat **trace**
Saturated fat **trace**
Sodium **25mg**

1 tsp	fresh lemon juice	1 tsp
125 g	cooked peeled prawns, finely chopped	4 oz
175 g	lemon sole fillets, or other white-fleshed fish	6 oz
2 tsp	dry vermouth	2 tsp
1	egg white	1
¼ tsp	salt	¼ tsp
3 tbsp	fromage frais	3 tbsp
3 tbsp	finely chopped spring onions	3 tbsp
	cayenne pepper	
6	thin slices white bread, trimmed to 9 cm (3 ½ inch) squares	6
4 tsp	white sesame seeds	4 tsp
	lettuce leaves, for garnish	

Add the lemon juice to the chopped prawns and set the mixture aside. In a food processor, purée the fish fillets with the vermouth, egg white and salt. Transfer the mixture from the processor to a bowl and set this in a larger bowl containing ice. Beat in the *fromage frais*, then gently stir in the chopped spring onions, cayenne pepper and chopped prawns. Meanwhile, preheat the oven to 200°C (400°F or Mark 6).

Toast the bread under the grill until lightly browned. Spread the prawn topping over the toast and cover with an even sprinkling of sesame seeds. Cut the toast slices into quarters, then cut each quarter diagonally into two triangles. Place the triangles on a baking sheet and bake them in the oven until they are golden-brown — 15 to 20 minutes. Serve the sesame-prawn toasts warm on a bed of salad leaves.

Goujons with Dill and Gherkin Dip

Serves 10
Working time: about 20 minutes
Total time: about 30 minutes

Calories **95**
Protein **9g**
Cholesterol **40mg**
Total fat **4g**
Saturated fat **3g**
Sodium **65mg**

125 g	medium oatmeal	4 oz
1	egg white	1
1 tsp	fresh lemon juice	1 tsp
1 tbsp	wholemeal flour	1 tbsp
¼ tsp	salt	¼ tsp
	freshly ground black pepper	
350 g	plaice fillets, skinned	12 oz
	Dill and gherkin dip	
175 g	crème fraîche	6 oz
175 g	thick Greek yogurt	6 oz
2	baby gherkins, finely chopped	2
1 tsp	finely cut fresh dill	1 tsp
1	lemon, grated rind only	1
	freshly ground black pepper	
	dill sprig, for garnish	

Preheat the oven to 220°C (425°F or Mark 7).

Put the oatmeal on a baking sheet and toast in the oven until it is golden-brown — 10 to 15 minutes; stir once or twice during this time, checking that the oatmeal does not burn. Remove it from the oven and allow it to cool.

To prepare the dip, mix together the *crème fraîche*, Greek yogurt, chopped gherkins, cut dill, lemon rind and some pepper. Transfer to a serving bowl and garnish with the sprig of dill.

Lightly whisk together the egg white and lemon juice; mix the oatmeal with the flour, salt and some pepper. Cut the plaice fillets into strips about 7.5 by 1 cm (3 by ½ inch). Dip the strips in the egg white, shake off excess, then roll them in the oatmeal mixture, coating them evenly. Place the strips on a non-stick baking sheet, and cook in the oven until the fish is tender and the outside lightly browned — 3 to 5 minutes. Serve the goujons hot, accompanied by the dip.

Bacon and Monkfish Rolls

Makes 18 rolls
Working time: about 15 minutes
Total time: about 45 minutes (includes marinating)

Per roll:
Calories **70**
Protein **6g**
Cholesterol **25mg**
Total fat **5g**
Saturated fat **2g**
Sodium **110mg**

500 g	trimmed, skinned and boned monkfish or halibut	1 lb
½ tsp	finely chopped fresh thyme	½ tsp
1	bay leaf, broken	1
	freshly ground black pepper	
1	lemon, juice only	1
9	thin rashers back bacon, trimmed of fat, cut in half lengthwise	9

Cut the fish into 18 cubes and put these in a bowl with the thyme, bay leaf, some pepper and the lemon juice.

Turn the cubes to coat them well and leave to marinate for at least 30 minutes. Meanwhile, soak 18 short wooden cocktail sticks in cold water for 10 minutes to prevent them from scorching under the grill.

Discard the pieces of bay leaf from the fish marinade. Wrap each cube of fish with a piece of bacon and thread on to a stick; ensure that the skewers pierce through the overlapping ends of bacon, to hold them together.

Cook the rolls under a hot grill for 4 to 5 minutes, turning once. Serve immediately.

Halibut Kievski

IN THIS VARIATION OF A TRADITIONAL RUSSIAN SNACK,
FISH — INSTEAD OF MEAT — IS WRAPPED ROUND LIGHTLY
BUTTERED PEAS.

Makes 24 kievski
Working time: about 15 minutes
Total time: about 1 hour and 20 minutes (includes chilling)

Per kievski:
Calories **20**
Protein **3g**
Cholesterol **10mg**
Total fat **1g**
Saturated fat **trace**
Sodium **25mg**

300 g	skinned and boned halibut or haddock, finely chopped	10 oz
½ tsp	very finely grated lemon rind	½ tsp
⅛ tsp	salt	⅛ tsp
	white pepper	
45 g	shelled peas, or frozen peas, thawed	1½ oz
7 g	unsalted butter	¼ oz
24	mange-tout (about 125 g/4 oz), strings removed	24

In a food processor, combine the halibut with the lemon rind, salt and some pepper until it forms a coarse paste. Chill the paste in the refrigerator for at least 1 hour.

Parboil the peas until they are barely tender — 3 to 4 minutes. Drain, refresh under cold water and drain again. (Frozen peas do not need parboiling.) Melt the butter in a small heavy-bottomed saucepan, remove from the heat and toss the peas in the butter.

Divide the paste into 24 portions. Roll a portion into a ball, then flatten it in the palm of your hand to form a disc about 7.5 cm (3 inches) in diameter. Place a few peas in the centre of the disc, then draw up the sides of the disc to form a ball around the peas. Make up more fish balls until you have used up all the paste and peas. Wrap a mange-tout round each ball and secure it with a cocktail stick.

Pour enough water into a saucepan to fill it about 2.5 cm (1 inch) deep. Set a lightly oiled stainless steel steamer in the pan and bring the water to the boil. Put the balls in the steamer, cover the pan and steam for 5 minutes. Serve immediately.

Pastry Crescents with a Fish Filling

Makes about 40 crescents
Working time: about 1 hour
Total time: about 2 hours and 20 minutes
(includes proving)

Per crescent:
Calories **90**
Protein **4g**
Cholesterol **20mg**
Total fat **4g**
Saturated fat **2g**
Sodium **40mg**

30 g	fresh yeast, or 15 g/½ oz dried yeast	1 oz
¼ litre	skimmed milk	8 fl oz
75 g	unsalted butter	2½ oz
500 g	strong plain flour	1 lb
½ tsp	salt	½ tsp
1	egg, plus a little beaten egg for brushing	1
2 tbsp	caraway seeds, for garnish	2 tbsp
	Fish filling	
½ tsp	unsalted butter	½ tsp
1	shallot or small onion, finely chopped	1
30 cl	unsalted fish stock (recipe, page 139)	½ pint
250 g	herring fillet	8 oz
250 g	salmon or salmon trout fillet	8 oz
2 tbsp	finely chopped fresh dill	2 tbsp

Cream the fresh yeast with 1 tablespoon of warm water and set aside for 10 minutes until activated; if using dried yeast, reconstitute according to the manufacturer's instructions. Warm the milk and butter in a saucepan. Sift the flour with the salt, make a well and beat in the milk and butter, yeast mixture and egg, using a wooden spoon. Turn the dough on to a floured surface, and knead until the dough feels elastic —

about 10 minutes. Cover with plastic film and set aside in a warm, draught-free place until it is double its original volume — 1 to 1½ hours.

Meanwhile, prepare the filling. Heat the butter in a frying pan over low heat; add the shallot and sauté gently for 10 minutes. Bring the stock to the boil in a saucepan, add the herring and salmon, and poach over low heat until the fish is just cooked through — about 3 minutes. Remove the fish from the pan with a slotted spoon, skin it and flake the flesh. Mix the fish and the dill into the shallots, and set aside to cool.

Knock back the yeast dough and knead it briefly. Divide the dough in half, and roll out the first half on a floured surface to form a rectangle approximately 40 by 28 cm (16 by 11 inches). Using a 6 cm (2½ inch) diameter round pastry cutter or the rim of an upturned glass, cut out about 20 circles from the dough. Place a small amount of the filling in the centre of each circle; wet the edges of the circles and bring the two halves together to form a semi-circle with the filling inside. Press to seal the edges, and bend the semi-circles to form crescents. Repeat the rolling, cutting and filling procedure with the remaining dough. Trimmings can be kneaded again and used to make more crescents.

Brush the beaten egg lightly over the crescents. Sprinkle the crescents with the caraway seeds and space them apart on lightly greased baking sheets, ensuring that they do not touch. Leave them to rise while the oven heats to 200°C (400°F or Mark 6). Place the crescents in the oven and bake until golden-brown — 10 to 12 minutes. Serve warm.

Lemon Sole Roulades

Makes 24 roulades
Working time: about 35 minutes
Total time: about 50 minutes

Per roulade:	12	large Chinese cabbage leaves	12
Calories **40**	2	lemon soles (about 350 g/12 oz each), cut into eight fillets and skinned	2
Protein **6g**			
Cholesterol **20mg**		lemon slices, for garnish	
Total fat **1g**		**Spicy rice filling**	
Saturated fat **trace**			
Sodium **45mg**	60 g	long-grain brown rice	2 oz
	¼ tsp	salt	¼ tsp
	60 g	button mushrooms, chopped	2 oz
	2	tomatoes, skinned, seeded (page 76) and chopped	2
	30 g	creamed coconut	1 oz
	½ tsp	curry powder	½ tsp
	1 tsp	grated fresh ginger root	1 tsp

To prepare the filling, add the rice and salt to 17.5 cl (6 fl oz) of water. Bring to the boil in a tightly covered saucepan, then reduce the heat and simmer until the rice is tender and all of the water is absorbed — about 20 minutes. Stir in the mushrooms, tomatoes, coconut, curry powder and ginger. Mix well and set aside.

Preheat the oven to 200°C (400°F or Mark 6). Soak 24 cocktail sticks in water for about 10 minutes to prevent them from scorching in the oven. Line a baking sheet with non-stick parchment paper.

Blanch the Chinese cabbage in boiling water for 15 seconds. Drain and refresh under cold running water, then drain again thoroughly. Cut each leaf lengthwise into two, removing and discarding the stem. Fold each cabbage piece to form a strip about 15 cm (6 inches) long by 2 cm (¾ inches) wide. Divide the rice filling into 24 portions and cover each leaf strip evenly with one portion of the filling.

Using a sharp knife, cut each sole fillet into three strips about 2 cm (¾ inch) wide. Place a strip of sole on each rice-topped leaf. Roll up the leaf neatly and secure with a cocktail stick.

Place the rolls on the prepared baking sheet and bake until the fish is tender and the leaves are still bright green — 5 to 6 minutes.

Serve warm, garnished with the lemon slices.

Seafood Sausages

Makes 30 sausages
Working (and total) time: about 30 minutes

Per sausage:
Calories **25**
Protein **2g**
Cholesterol **10mg**
Total fat **2g**
Saturated fat **trace**
Sodium **65mg**

90 g	lemon sole fillet, skinned	3 oz
175 g	monkfish fillet	6 oz
125 g	salmon tailpiece fillet	4 oz
1	egg white	1
1 tsp	green peppercorns, coarsely crushed	1 tsp
¼ tsp	grated lemon rind	¼ tsp
1 tsp	salt	1 tsp
2 tbsp	virgin olive oil	2 tbsp
	lemon slices or wedges, for garnish	

Roughly chop the lemon sole, monkfish and half of the salmon. In a food processor, process the chopped fish for a few seconds, then add the egg white and process until the mixture becomes just paste-like. Chop the remaining salmon finely and mix it into the fish paste along with the peppercorns, lemon rind and salt.

Divide the fish paste into 30 walnut-sized portions and roll each piece into a sausage shape. Heat the oil in a heavy frying pan over medium heat until it is hot, but not smoking. Fry the sausages, turning all the time, until well browned — 1½ to 2 minutes. Serve garnished with slices or wedges of lemon.

Oiling Griddles and Frying Pans

While the higher fat content of more traditional recipes allows you to cook on the well-seasoned surface of a griddle or heavy frying pan without using additional fat, the low-fat recipes in this book often require a slightly different approach to guard against sticking.

A non-stick griddle or frying pan that has been maintained according to the manufacturer's instructions need not be oiled. However, if either is beginning to show signs of wear — particularly scratches — it is a good idea to coat the surface with a film of oil. Pour ¼ teaspoon of safflower oil on to the griddle or into the frying pan and rub it all over the bottom with a paper towel. Do not discard the towel; it will have absorbed enough oil to allow you to coat the surface several times, as needed, during the cooking process.

A well-seasoned, heavy griddle or frying pan that does not have a non-stick surface should be treated in the same way, but with 1 teaspoon of oil instead of ¼ teaspoon. In both cases, most of the oil will be retained by the towel and thus have little effect on the final calorie count.

Spicy Chicken Wings

Makes 24 pieces
Working time: about 30 minutes
Total time: about 5 hours (includes marinating)

Per piece:			
Calories **15**	12	chicken wings	12
Protein **2g**	15 cl	plain low-fat yogurt	¼ pint
Cholesterol **10mg**	1 tbsp	fresh lemon juice	1 tbsp
Total fat **trace**	1 tbsp	honey	1 tbsp
Saturated fat **trace**	2.5 cm	piece fresh ginger root, grated	1 inch
Sodium **45mg**	1 tsp	ground turmeric	1 tsp
	1 tbsp	boemboe sesate, or ¾ tsp each ground coriander, cumin, galangal and lemon grass	1 tbsp
	½ tsp	salt	½ tsp
		curly endive or lettuce, for garnish	

Cut off the chicken wing tips, and either discard or reserve them for stock-making. Separate each wing into two at the joint, and trim off loose skin with scissors or a sharp knife.

Combine the yogurt, lemon juice, honey, ginger, turmeric, boemboe sesate and salt, and spread the mixture over the chicken pieces. Leave to marinate in a cool place for at least 4 hours, preferably overnight.

Preheat the oven to 230°C (450°F or Mark 8).

Remove the chicken pieces from the marinade and arrange them in a baking dish or ovenproof casserole. Bake the chicken in the oven for about 15 minutes. Serve slightly cooled, for ease of handling, on a bed of curly endive or a chiffonade of lettuce.

EDITOR'S NOTE: *The chicken pieces may also be cooked under a hot grill, turning at least once until they are well browned — about 15 minutes.*

Aromatic Chicken Kofta

Makes 30 kofta
Working time: about 45 minutes
Total time: about 1 hour

Per kofta:
Calories **20**
Protein **2g**
Cholesterol **5mg**
Total fat **1g**
Saturated fat **trace**
Sodium **30mg**

60 g	burghul	2 oz
12	cardamom pods, seeds only	12
250 g	boneless chicken breast, skinned and chopped	8 oz
1 tsp	ground coriander	1 tsp
½ tsp	ground cumin	½ tsp
45 g	mint, finely chopped	1 ½ oz
1	garlic clove, crushed	1
½ tsp	salt	½ tsp
	freshly ground black pepper	
2 tsp	virgin olive oil	2 tsp
	lemon and lime wedges, for garnish	

Put the burghul in a small saucepan and add water to cover the burghul by about 1 cm (½ inch). Bring to the boil, then cover the pan and simmer until the burghul is soft and all the water has been absorbed — about 15 minutes. Set aside to cool.

Set a heavy frying pan over high heat, add the cardamom seeds and cook until they start to pop — about 1 minute. Finely grind the seeds, using a pestle and mortar or rolling pin.

Preheat the grill to high. In a food processor, combine the chicken, ground cardamom seeds, coriander, cumin, mint, garlic, salt and a little pepper for a few seconds to form a paste. Add the chicken paste to the burghul and mix together, then form the mixture into 30 small balls. Brush the balls with the oil, and cook under the grill until they are crisp and golden, turning frequently — 4 to 5 minutes. Serve the kofta hot, accompanied by the lemon and lime wedges.

Miniature Spring Rolls

Makes 32 spring rolls
Working (and total) time: about 1 hour and 30 minutes

Per spring roll:
Calories **25**
Protein **2g**
Cholesterol **10mg**
Total fat **1g**
Saturated fat **0g**
Sodium **30mg**

1 ½ tsp	cornflour	1 ½ tsp
1 tsp	dry sherry or sake	1 tsp
½ tsp	salt	½ tsp
	white pepper	
125 g	chicken breast meat, cut into fine strips	4 oz
7 g	cloud-ear mushrooms, soaked in hot water for 20 minutes	¼ oz
1	egg	1
2 tbsp	safflower oil	2 tbsp
1	garlic clove, finely chopped	1
1 cm	piece fresh ginger root, finely chopped	½ inch
90 g	bean sprouts	3 oz
1	small sweet green pepper, seeded, deribbed and finely shredded	1
60 g	carrots, finely shredded	2 oz
8	sheets phyllo pastry, each about 45 by 30 cm (18 by 12 inches)	8
1	sweet yellow pepper, for garnish (optional)	1
Fruit dipping sauce		
¼ litre	pineapple juice	8 fl oz
¼ tsp	finely chopped fresh ginger root	¼ tsp
½	lemon, grated rind and strained juice	½
1 tsp	low-sodium soy sauce or shoyu	1 tsp
¼ tsp	tomato paste	¼ tsp
1 tsp	cornflour, dissolved in 1 ½ tsp water	1 tsp
2	spring onions, finely chopped	2

In a shallow dish, mix the cornflour with the sherry or sake, ¼ tsp of the salt and a little white pepper. Coat the chicken with this mixture and leave to stand for 10 minutes. Strain the cloud-ear mushrooms, squeeze dry and shred finely.

Beat the egg until frothy. Heat a small non-stick frying pan over medium heat and pour in the egg to make a thin omelette. Allow the omelette to cool, then cut it into fine shreds.

Place a wok over high heat until very hot, add ½ teaspoon of the oil and stir-fry the chicken for 20 to 30 seconds. Remove the chicken from the wok and keep it warm. Add 1 teaspoon of the oil to the wok and fry the garlic and ginger for 10 seconds, then add the mushrooms and stir-fry for 20 seconds. Finally, add the bean sprouts, green pepper and carrots, and stir-fry for a further 20 seconds, adding the remaining salt and a little pepper half way through. Remove the wok from the heat. Leave to cool, then mix in the shredded omelette and the chicken.

Preheat the oven to 200°C (400°F or Mark 6).

Divide the filling mixture into 32 parts. Keeping the sheets of phyllo pastry stacked, cut each into four strips measuring about 11 by 30 cm (4½ by 12 inches).

Cover the stacks of phyllo you are not working on with a dampened tea towel to prevent them from drying out and becoming brittle. Brush one strip of phyllo lightly with oil and place a portion of filling along one of the shorter ends, leaving 1 cm (½ inch) uncovered on either side. Roll the phyllo round the filling a couple of times, fold the uncovered edges in, and continue rolling until you reach the other end. Place the roll seam side down on a lightly oiled or non-stick baking sheet. Repeat with the remaining phyllo strips and filling. Bake the rolls, turning once, until they are golden-brown — 15 to 20 minutes.

Meanwhile, prepare the sauce. In a non-reactive pan, reduce the pineapple juice by half over high heat. Add the ginger and the lemon rind and juice, and cook gently for 1 minute. Add the soy sauce, tomato paste and cornflour, and heat through. Remove the pan from the heat, and add the spring onions.

Slice off the top of the yellow pepper and remove the ribs and seeds to make a container for the dipping sauce; alternatively, spoon the sauce into a bowl. Serve the spring rolls on a warmed serving platter, accompanied by the dipping sauce.

EDITOR'S NOTE: *The omelette will absorb any moisture from the vegetables during cooking and ensure that the pastry remains crisp. You can substitute 30 g (1 oz) of lightly toasted breadcrumbs, but the egg adds more flavour to the rolls.*

Turkey Twists

Makes 20 twists
Working time: about 30 minutes
Total time: about 3 hours (includes marinating)

Per twist:			
Calories **25**	300 g	boneless turkey breasts, skinned	10 oz
Protein **5g**	125 g	cranberries	4 oz
Cholesterol **10mg**		thinly pared lime rind, cut into 20 leaf shapes	
Total fat **trace**			
Saturated fat **trace**	2 tsp	clear honey	2 tsp
Sodium **50mg**		**Lime-ginger marinade**	
	1 tbsp	freshly grated ginger root	1 tbsp
	1	garlic clove, crushed	1
	1 tbsp	clear honey	1 tbsp
	1	lime, grated rind and 1 tbsp juice only	1
	45 g	plain low-fat yogurt	1½ oz
	½ tsp	salt	½ tsp
		Tabasco sauce	

To make the marinade, put the grated ginger, garlic, honey, grated lime rind and juice, yogurt, salt and a few drops of Tabasco sauce in a bowl and stir well until evenly blended. Slice the turkey thinly, then cut the slices into strips measuring about 12 by 1 cm (5 by ½ inch). Place the strips in the marinade, and turn to coat evenly. Set aside to marinate for 2 to 3 hours.

Soak 20 wooden kebab skewers in water for 10 to 15 minutes to prevent them from scorching under the grill during cooking.

Place the lime leaves, cranberries and honey in a small saucepan with about 2 tablespoons of water, and cook very gently until the cranberries begin to soften — 3 to 4 minutes. Drain the cranberries and lime leaves and set aside.

Thread each turkey strip on to one end of a skewer to form a continuous double "S" shape, skewering a cranberry between each loop of the "S".

Line a baking sheet with non-stick parchment paper. Arrange the turkey twists on the sheet and cook under a hot grill for 12 to 15 minutes, turning once, until the turkey is tender and the coating a darker colour.

Garnish the end of each skewer with a lime leaf and arrange the twists on a serving plate.

Pork Phyllo Pastries

Makes 12 pastries
Working time: about 20 minutes
Total time: about 1 hour and 10 minutes
(includes marinating)

Per pastry:			
Calories **55**	300 g	pork fillet, trimmed of fat, finely chopped	10 oz
Protein **4g**	1 tbsp	dry sherry or rice wine	1 tbsp
Cholesterol **15mg**	1 tbsp	low-sodium soy sauce or shoyu	1 tbsp
Total fat **3g**	1 tsp	finely chopped fresh ginger root	1 tsp
Saturated fat **2g**	3 tbsp	chopped spring onions	3 tbsp
Sodium **15mg**		freshly ground black pepper	
	3	sheets phyllo pastry, each about 45 by 30 cm (18 by 12 inches)	3
	30 g	unsalted butter, melted	1 oz

Place the chopped pork in a shallow non-reactive bowl with the sherry or rice wine, soy sauce, ginger, spring onions and some freshly ground pepper, and leave to marinate for 20 minutes.

Preheat the oven to 200°C (400°F or Mark 6). Cut each phyllo sheet into quarters and fold each quarter in half crosswise. Line 12 cups of a deep bun tin tray with the phyllo, leaving the edges to overhang. Divide the pork mixture among the cups. Brush the overhanging phyllo edges with some of the melted butter, then fold the edges over the mixture to resemble the petals of a flower; twist slightly to keep them in place. Brush the phyllo again with the remaining melted butter, then cover the tray with aluminium foil and cook in the oven for 30 minutes. About 10 minutes before the end of the cooking time, remove the foil to allow the phyllo to brown. Serve the pastries hot.

EDITOR'S NOTE: *These pork pastries may also be served at room temperature.*

Thai-Style Parcels

THE INGREDIENTS FOR THIS DISH ARE PREPARED BY
THE COOK AND PRESENTED AT TABLE FOR EACH GUEST
TO ASSEMBLE INDIVIDUALLY.

Makes 48 parcels
Working time: about 1 hour
Total time: about 4 hours (includes chilling and marinating)

Per parcel:
Calories **30**
Protein **3g**
Cholesterol **10mg**
Total fat **2g**
Saturated fat **1g**
Sodium **25mg**

350 g	lean fillet of beef, trimmed of fat and chilled in the freezer until firm (about 1 hour)	12 oz
350 g	boneless chicken breast, skinned	12 oz
1	Chinese cabbage, washed, dried and finely shredded	1
1	large lettuce, leaves washed and dried	1
½	cucumber, peeled in alternate strips with a cannelle knife, halved lengthwise and thinly sliced	½
1	bunch fresh coriander, leaves only	1
1	bunch fresh mint, large stalks removed	1
1	bunch fresh basil, leaves only	1
48	rice-paper wrappers (about 6 inches/15 cm in diameter)	48
1 tbsp	groundnut oil	1 tbsp
	freshly ground black pepper	
Spicy marinade		
30 g	tamarind paste, dissolved in 15 cl (¼ pint) water for 15 minutes	1 oz
1 tsp	sambal oelek	1 tsp
1 tbsp	ketjap manis or low-sodium soy sauce	1 tbsp
2 tsp	nam pla, or 1 tsp anchovy purée	2 tsp
3	garlic cloves, crushed	3
4 cm	piece fresh ginger root, peeled and finely shredded	1½ inch
Lemon glaze		
4 tbsp	fresh lemon juice	4 tbsp
2 tbsp	ketjap manis or low-sodium soy sauce	2 tbsp
1 tsp	molasses sugar	1 tsp
Dipping sauce		
10 cl	fresh lemon juice	3½ fl oz
4 tbsp	ketjap manis or low-sodium soy sauce	4 tbsp
2 tsp	sambal oelek	2 tsp
1 cm	piece fresh ginger root, peeled and finely shredded	½ inch
1	small stick fresh lemon grass, finely chopped	1

To make the marinade, strain the tamarind liquid and discard the solids. Add the sambal oelek, ketjap manis, nam pla, garlic and ginger to the liquid and stir well to blend the ingredients. Divide the marinade between two shallow dishes. Slice the beef very thinly across the grain, then cut the slices into strips about 1 cm (½ inch) wide. Cut the chicken breast into thin strips of the same width. Place the beef in one of the marinade dishes, and the chicken in the other; stir to coat the strips evenly, and leave to marinate in a cool place for 3 hours.

Shortly before serving, combine the glaze ingredients with 2 tablespoons of water in a small saucepan and boil until reduced to about 3 tablespoons — 3 to 5 minutes.

Meanwhile, make up the dipping sauce by combining all the ingredients with 4 tablespoons of water. Pour the sauce into dipping bowls. Arrange the Chinese cabbage, lettuce leaves and cucumber slices on a serving platter, and the coriander, mint and basil on a second platter. Set out the rice-paper wrappers and bowls of tepid water for dipping the wrappers.

In a wok or a wide, heavy frying pan, heat the oil until sizzling. Take the beef strips out of the marinade and sear them for about 20 seconds, stirring and tossing the meat with a spatula. Remove the beef and keep warm. Cook the chicken strips in the wok until the flesh is no longer translucent — about 45 seconds.

Arrange the beef and chicken on separate serving dishes, and brush with the glaze. Serve immediately, with the raw ingredients, pepper and sauce, for each guest to make up into parcels and dip *(below)*.

EDITOR'S NOTE: *Less familiar ingredients, described in the glossary on pages 140-141, are available from Oriental grocers.*

Rice Paper Packages

MAKING UP A PARCEL. Dip a rice-paper wrapper in a bowl of tepid water, gently shake off excess water and place the softened wrapper on the palm of your hand or on a small plate. Place small quantities of ingredients on the centre of the wrapper, and fold the edges over the filling to enclose it. Then dip the finished parcel in the sauce (above).

Thai Skewers

Makes 18 skewers
Working time: about 25 minutes
Total time: about 2 hours and 40 minutes
(includes chilling)

Per skewer:			
Calories **55**	250 g	pork fillet or escalope, trimmed of fat	8 oz
Protein **6g**			
Cholesterol **40mg**	350 g	raw prawns, shelled and deveined	12 oz
Total fat **2g**	100 g	white crab meat, picked over	3 ½ oz
Saturated fat **trace**	3	garlic cloves	3
Sodium **90mg**	2.5 cm	piece fresh ginger root, peeled	1 inch
	½ tsp	fresh lime juice	½ tsp
	¼ tsp	grated lime rind	¼ tsp
	1 tsp	ground galangal	1 tsp
	1 tsp	ground lemon grass	1 tsp
	3 tbsp	chopped fresh coriander	3 tbsp
	1 tbsp	chopped fresh basil	1 tbsp
	½ tsp	salt	½ tsp
		freshly ground black pepper	
	1 tsp	arrowroot	1 tsp
	½	beaten egg white	½
	1	papaya, peeled and cut into 1 cm (½ inch) cubes	1
	1 tbsp	safflower oil	1 tbsp

Aromatic dip

2 tbsp	low-sodium soy sauce or shoyu	2 tbsp
1 tbsp	fresh lime juice	1 tbsp
1 tbsp	molasses sugar	1 tbsp
1	garlic clove	1
1 cm	piece fresh ginger root, peeled	½ inch
	fine strips of fresh chili pepper (caution, page 18)	

Mince the pork finely in a food processor, then transfer it to a large bowl. Process the prawns to a fine paste and add them to the minced pork, then process and add the white crab meat. Mix the pork and shellfish together well with your hands.

Using a garlic press, squeeze the juice from the garlic and ginger into the pork and shellfish mixture. Add the lime juice and rind, galangal, lemon grass, coriander, basil, salt and a generous grinding of black pepper. Mix the ingredients together. Stir the arrowroot into the egg white until no lumps remain, and blend the arrowroot and egg white into the pork and fish mixture. Chill for at least 2 hours.

To make the dip, combine the soy sauce and lime juice with 2 tablespoons of water in a small bowl, and dissolve the molasses sugar in the mixture. Using a garlic press, squeeze the juice from the garlic and fresh ginger into the mixture. Add the chili peppers and pour into a serving bowl.

Preheat the grill to medium. Soak 18 wooden satay sticks or skewers in water for about 10 minutes to prevent them from burning under the grill.

Form the chilled pork and shellfish mixture into 54 small balls, each about 2 cm (¾ inch) in diameter. Thread three balls on to each skewer, alternating them with cubes of papaya.

Brush a grill pan lightly with a little of the safflower oil, and arrange the skewers in a single layer in the pan. Brush the balls and the papaya cubes lightly with the remaining oil. Cook the skewers for about 10 minutes, turning once, until they are golden-brown. Serve immediately, accompanied by the dip.

Stuffed Pasta Rings

Makes 24 rings
Working time: about 20 minutes
Total time: about 30 minutes

Per ring:	4	thin slices wholemeal bread, crusts removed	4
Calories **40**			
Protein **2g**	3	cannelloni tubes (about 60 g/2 oz)	3
Cholesterol **trace**			
Total fat **1g**	90 g	low-fat mozzarella, grated	3 oz
Saturated fat **trace**	3 tbsp	medium oatmeal	3 tbsp
Sodium **70mg**	30 g	very thinly sliced prosciutto, for garnish	1 oz
		flat-leaf parsley, for garnish	
	Tomato and basil filling		
	4	spring onions, finely chopped	4
	1	small garlic clove, crushed	1
	300 g	tomatoes, skinned, seeded (page 76) and chopped	10 oz
	2 tsp	tomato paste	2 tsp
	1 tsp	finely chopped fresh basil	1 tsp
	½ tsp	clear honey	½ tsp
		freshly ground black pepper	

To prepare the tomato and basil filling, place the spring onions, garlic, tomatoes and tomato paste in a small heavy-bottomed saucepan. Cook over medium heat, stirring occasionally, until the mixture is pulpy and thick. Stir in the basil, honey and a little freshly ground pepper, remove from the heat and set aside.

Roll out the slices of bread thinly with a rolling pin, then cut six rounds from each slice using a 2.5 cm (1 inch) plain cutter. Toast the bread rounds under a hot grill until browned. Arrange them evenly, spaced apart, on a baking sheet.

Cook the cannelloni in plenty of lightly salted boiling water until just tender — 8 to 10 minutes. Drain them and rinse well under cold running water, then thread each pasta tube on to a wooden spoon handle to prevent it from closing up.

Mix the grated mozzarella and oatmeal together. Using the round cutter, cut out 24 rounds of prosciutto; set the rounds aside for a garnish.

Cut each pasta tube into eight rings and place the rings on the toast rounds. Divide the mozzarella and oatmeal mixture into two; distribute one portion among the pasta rings, a little into each ring. Divide the tomato filling equally among the pasta rings, then sprinkle with the remaining mozzarella mixture. Place the baking sheet under a hot grill and grill until the mozzarella topping begins to brown — 3 to 4 minutes.

Garnish each canapé with a folded piece of prosciutto and a parsley leaf. Serve warm.

EDITOR'S NOTE: *These pasta canapés may also be served at room temperature.*

Veal with Apricot and Nut Stuffing

Makes 32 slices
Working time: about 15 minutes
Total time: about 1 hour and 25 minutes (includes soaking)

Per slice:
Calories **45**
Protein **5g**
Cholesterol **15mg**
Total fat **2g**
Saturated fat **1g**
Sodium **40mg**

4	veal escalopes (about 175 g/6 oz each), beaten thin	4
1 tsp	safflower oil	1 tsp
	coriander sprigs, for garnish	
	Apricot and nut stuffing	
125 g	dried apricots, soaked in boiling water for at least 1 hour, chopped	4 oz
1 tbsp	finely chopped spring onion	1 tbsp
60 g	unsalted cashew nuts, finely chopped	2 oz
2 tsp	chopped fresh coriander	2 tsp
6	cardamom pods, crushed seeds only	6
4 tbsp	fresh orange juice	4 tbsp
¼ tsp	salt	¼ tsp
	freshly ground black pepper	

Preheat the oven to 200°C (400°F or Mark 6). Line a baking sheet with non-stick parchment paper.

To make the stuffing, place the chopped apricots, spring onion, cashew nuts, coriander, cardamom seeds, orange juice, salt and some freshly ground pepper in a heavy-bottomed saucepan. Cook over a moderate heat, stirring occasionally, until the mixture softens — about 2 minutes.

Cut the veal escalopes in half across their width. Divide the stuffing among the pieces of veal, spreading it evenly to the edges. Neatly roll up each piece and secure it with two cocktail sticks or small skewers. Place the rolls on the baking sheet and lightly brush the meat with the oil.

Bake the stuffed rolls in the centre of the oven until the veal is lightly browned — 5 to 8 minutes. Allow the rolls to cool for a few minutes, then remove the cocktail sticks and cut each roll into four slices. Serve immediately, garnished with the coriander sprigs.

EDITOR'S NOTE: *The apricots may be replaced with soaked dried peaches, apples or prunes, or a mixture of dried fruit. This snack may also be served at room temperature.*

Spiced Steak Phyllo Boats

Makes 30 boats
Working (and total) time: about 50 minutes

Per boat:			

Per boat:
Calories **40**
Protein **3g**
Cholesterol **10mg**
Total fat **2g**
Saturated fat **1g**
Sodium **10mg**

6	sheets phyllo pastry, each about 45 by 30 cm (18 by 12 inches)	6
1½ tbsp	virgin olive oil	1½ tbsp
1	small onion, very finely chopped	1
30 g	pine-nuts	1 oz
2	garlic cloves, crushed	2
1 tsp	ground cumin	1 tsp
1 tsp	ground cardamom	1 tsp
⅛ tsp	cayenne pepper	⅛ tsp
¼ tsp	ground cinnamon	¼ tsp
125 g	mushrooms, finely chopped	4 oz
45 g	raisins, chopped	1½ oz
250 g	rump steak, trimmed of fat, finely minced	8 oz
¼ tsp	salt	¼ tsp
	freshly ground black pepper	
1 tbsp	finely cut chives	1 tbsp

Preheat the oven to 220°C (425°F or Mark 7).

Lay out three sheets of phyllo pastry, one on top of another, on a work surface. Using an inverted 11 by 5 cm (4½ by 2 inch) boat-shaped tartlet tin as a guide, cut out oval shapes from the sheets. Fit the ovals into 9 by 4 cm (3½ by 1½ inch) boat-shaped tins, pressing the phyllo firmly into position. Trim the pointed ends into shape with scissors. Repeat with the remaining phyllo sheets until you have filled 30 tartlet tins. Place the tins on baking sheets and bake in the oven until the pastry is golden-brown — 6 to 8 minutes. Carefully remove the phyllo boats from the tins and set them on wire racks to cool.

To make the filling, heat half the oil in a heavy frying pan. Add the onion and cook gently until it is softened, but not browned — 5 to 6 minutes. Add the pine-nuts, garlic, cumin, cardamom, cayenne pepper and cinnamon. Cook for 2 to 3 minutes, then add the mushrooms and cook until they are softened and most of the liquid has evaporated — 6 to 8 minutes. Stir in the raisins. Remove the mushroom mixture from the pan to a plate, and set aside.

Heat the remaining oil in the frying pan until it begins to smoke. Add the steak and stir-fry it just long enough for the meat to change colour — do not overcook. Return the mushroom mixture to the pan and heat through. Season with the salt and some pepper.

Spoon the filling into the phyllo boats and sprinkle with the chives. Serve warm.

EDITOR'S NOTE: *The phyllo cases may be prepared ahead of time and stored in an airtight container.*

Making Sausages

1 *PREPARING THE CASINGS. Roll one length of casing on to the nozzle of a mincer, as here, or a food processor, funnel or piping bag, leaving 5 cm (2 inches) hanging loose. Fill the mincer's bowl with the prepared stuffing and turn the handle. When the stuffing just emerges from the nozzle, tie a knot in the casing.*

2 *FILLING THE CASING. Continue turning the handle to fill the casing; use a wooden spoon to push the meat down into the mincer. As the stuffing is fed into the casing, gradually slip the casing off the nozzle; use your fingers to prevent overstretching and eliminate any air bubbles.*

3 *FORMING LINKS. When only about 5 cm (2 inches) of the casing remains to be filled, slip it off the nozzle and knot it. Roll it on a work surface to even out the stuffing. To form links, twist the lengths through three or four turns at intervals of about 2.5 cm (1 inch), as shown above.*

Little Beef Sausages with Horseradish

Makes about 60 sausages
Working time: about 35 minutes
Total time: about 1 hour and 45 minutes (includes soaking)

Per sausage:			
Calories **25**	90 g	fresh brown breadcrumbs	3 oz
Protein **3g**	2	shallots, finely chopped	2
Cholesterol **5mg**	1	garlic clove, crushed	1
Total fat **1g**	1 tbsp	chopped parsley	1 tbsp
Saturated fat **trace**	2 tsp	chopped fresh thyme	2 tsp
Sodium **35mg**	1 tsp	chopped fresh sage	1 tsp

500 g	lean beef, finely minced	1 lb
30 g	medium oatmeal	1 oz
2 tsp	Dijon mustard	2 tsp
½ tsp	salt	½ tsp
	freshly ground black pepper	
2	egg whites	2
2 metres	natural lamb sausage casings, soaked in acidulated water for 1 hour	6 feet
1 tsp	safflower oil	1 tsp
Horseradish dip		
1 tbsp	red wine vinegar	1 tbsp
1 tsp	Dijon mustard	1 tsp
1 tsp	fresh lemon juice	1 tsp
¼ tsp	salt	¼ tsp
	freshly ground black pepper	
15 cl	plain low-fat yogurt	¼ pint
1 ½ tbsp	grated horseradish	1 ½ tbsp

Preheat the oven to 200°C (400°F or Mark 6). Lightly brush a non-stick dish or baking tin with oil.

In a large bowl, combine the breadcrumbs, shallots, garlic, parsley, thyme and sage. Add the beef and mix well. Add the oatmeal, mustard, salt, some pepper and the egg whites, and mix together all the ingredients.

Unravel the sausage casings and cut them in two. Roll one end of a length of casing over the spout of a funnel or tap and run cold water through it to open it out, then rinse the other length in the same way. Drain the casings. Make up the 2.5 cm (1 inch) sausages as shown *(above)*.

Place the linked sausages in the dish or baking tin and brush them lightly with the safflower oil. Bake in the oven for 10 to 15 minutes, until golden-brown. While the sausages are cooking, mix together the ingredients for the dip in a small serving bowl.

Cut through the links with kitchen scissors and place the sausages on a serving plate. Serve immediately with the horseradish dip.

EDITOR'S NOTE: *Natural sausage casings — the cleansed intestines of lamb, pig or ox — can be ordered from your butcher or from specialist suppliers. Lamb casings are usually used for small sausages. Pork, veal, lamb or a mixture of meats may be substituted for the beef.*

Sausage Rolls

Makes 40 rolls
Working time: about 1 hour
Total time: about 1 hour and 25 minutes

Per roll:
Calories **50**
Protein **2g**
Cholesterol **5mg**
Total fat **3g**
Saturated fat **1g**
Sodium **80mg**

20	thin slices wholemeal bread	20
2 tbsp	prepared English or Dijon mustard	2 tbsp
60 g	polyunsaturated margarine	2 oz
2 tsp	tomato paste	2 tsp
2	garlic cloves, crushed	2
Pork sausage-meat		
400 g	pork shoulder, trimmed of excess fat	14 oz
1	onion, roughly chopped	1
60 g	fresh wholemeal breadcrumbs	2 oz
30 g	polyunsaturated margarine	1 oz
¼ tsp	salt	¼ tsp
	freshly ground black pepper	
2 tsp	mixed dried herbs	2 tsp

To make the sausage-meat, cut the pork into strips and pass the meat and onion through the fine blade of a mincer into a bowl. Mix in the breadcrumbs, margarine, salt, some pepper and the herbs, then pass the mixture through the mincer once again.

Preheat the oven to 220°C (425°F or Mark 7). Grease several baking sheets.

Remove the crusts from the bread, then roll each slice with a rolling pin to make it pliable. Set aside.

Divide the sausage-meat mixture into five equal portions, then shape each portion into a sausage shape about 40 cm (16 inches) long. Cut each sausage into four equal pieces.

Spread each slice of bread with the mustard. Put a length of sausage-meat on one edge of each slice. Roll the bread up to enclose the sausage-meat, ending with the join underneath.

Put the margarine, tomato paste and garlic into a small bowl and beat well together until very soft. Brush the garlic mixture evenly over the sausage rolls. Cut each roll in half. Place the sausage rolls, seam side down, on the prepared baking sheets and cook in the oven until they are golden-brown and crisp — about 25 minutes. Serve warm.

Bacon and Date Pinwheels

Makes 40 pinwheels
Working time: about 15 minutes
Total time: about 20 minutes

Per pinwheel:
Calories **40**
Protein **2g**
Cholesterol **5mg**
Total fat **2g**
Saturated fat **1g**
Sodium **125mg**

10	large thin slices wholemeal bread, crusts removed	10
10	fresh dates, halved and stoned	10
10	thin rashers lean back bacon, fat trimmed, halved lengthwise	10
1 tsp	clear honey	1 tsp
	parsley sprigs, for garnish	
	Tomato filling	
300 g	tomatoes, skinned, seeded (page 76) and chopped	10 oz
1 tsp	tomato paste	1 tsp
1	shallot, finely chopped	1
1	bay leaf	1
	freshly ground black pepper	

To prepare the tomato filling, put the tomatoes, tomato paste, shallot, bay leaf and some pepper into a small heavy-bottomed saucepan. Cook over moderate heat, stirring occasionally, until the mixture has thickened. Remove from the heat and set aside.

Preheat the oven to 200°C (400°F or Mark 6). Roll out each slice of bread thinly with a rolling pin and trim into a neat rectangle with its shorter sides the length of two dates laid end to end.

Take one piece of bread and spread it sparingly with some of the tomato filling. Lay two date halves end to end along a short edge of the slice and roll up the bread firmly. Cut the bread roll in half between the two dates. Wrap a piece of bacon round one of the rolls, ensuring that the bacon covers the seam of the bread, and secure with two wooden cocktail sticks. Cut the roll in half between the cocktail sticks to make two pinwheels. Wrap and cut the other roll.

Repeat this process with the remaining bread slices, dates and bacon to make 40 pinwheels. Place the pinwheels on a baking sheet lined with parchment paper. Warm the honey in a small saucepan and lightly brush each roll with it, then bake the pinwheels in the oven until the bacon is cooked — 5 to 8 minutes. Arrange the pinwheels on a serving plate and garnish with the parsley sprigs.

EDITOR'S NOTE: *You can vary this recipe by using soaked prunes or fresh apricots instead of dates.*

Ox Heart Brochettes

Makes 16 brochettes
Working time: about 15 minute
Total time: about 1 day (includes marinating)

Per brochette:
Calories **50**
Protein **8g**
Cholesterol **35mg**
Total fat **2g**
Saturated fat **1g**
Sodium **95mg**

500 g	ox heart, trimmed of fat	1 lb
5	garlic cloves, crushed	5
3	fresh red or green chili peppers (caution, page 18), seeded, finely chopped	3
2 tsp	hot chili powder	2 tsp
2 tsp	safflower oil	2 tsp
3 tbsp	red wine vinegar	3 tbsp
½ tsp	salt	½ tsp
	freshly ground black pepper	

Cut the heart into 2.5 cm (1 inch) cubes — you should have about 48 cubes. Mix the garlic, chilies, chili pow-der, oil, vinegar, salt and some pepper together in a large dish. Add the ox heart cubes and turn to coat them well. Cover the dish and leave to marinate in the refrigerator for about 24 hours.

Ten minutes before grilling the ox heart, soak 16 wooden skewers, about 20 cm (8 inches) long, in water to prevent them from scorching under the grill. Preheat the grill to high. Thread the cubes of ox heart on to the skewers, reserving any marinade left in the dish, and grill the brochettes for 2 to 3 minutes on one side. Turn, brush with the reserved marinade, and cook the brochettes for a further 2 minutes. The meat should be well browned on all sides.

EDITOR'S NOTE: *Cubes of lean grilling steak may be substi-tuted for the ox heart in this recipe.*

3 *Tomatoes, prosciutto and low-fat mozzarella cheese fill the baked dough squares known in Italy as calzone (recipe, page 123).*

Sandwiches and Hearty Snacks

According to legend, in 1792 the gambling Earl of Sandwich, too engrossed at the card table to stop for dinner, called for meat served between two slices of bread, and thus gave his name to an entire culinary genre. While retaining the essence of the Earl's original concept, the sandwiches presented in this chapter offer multiple variations on his theme to suit endless occasions. Wrought into pinwheels with mushrooms or watercress *(page 106)*, they make a filling diversion for a grand reception; thin and crustless, with a cucumber filling *(page 104)*, they grace the traditional English tea table; and as chunky baguettes filled with hot prawns and garlic *(page 114)*, they provide a filling pre-theatre supper.

Some sandwiches that follow do away with the top layer of bread. For a sustaining hot snack, a slice of toast can be topped simply with a savoury mushroom mixture *(page 118)* or, Catalan-style, with crushed tomatoes and ham *(page 112)*. For a buffet lunch or dinner, Danish-style open sandwiches *(page 110 to 111)* offer another decorative variation on the theme.

Whatever the context, the key to a successful sandwich is the bread used to make it. Home-made bread is hard to surpass *(page 10)*, but more convenient are the wide variety of commercial breads now available: wholemeal and granary loaves; rye bread flecked with caraway or cumin seeds; and crusty rolls and baguettes. Mexican tortillas and Italian pizza bases make novel variations, while the increasingly popular Middle Eastern pitta, warmed through and slit open, makes a capacious pouch that is virtually all crust and very little crumb.

While unnecessary fat has been kept to a minimum in these recipes, bear in mind that butter or margarine is an integral part of most cold sandwiches, acting as a protective barrier between the bread and the filling. To maximize its benefit while minimizing your intake, spread it as thinly but as evenly as possible. In the odd exception, such as the Provençal sandwich on page 113, butter is omitted altogether so the juice-soaked bread becomes as much a feature as the filling.

Most sandwiches can be prepared in advance, provided they are wrapped in plastic film immediately to prevent them from drying out. Open sandwiches, however, should be assembled just before serving so as to maximize the appeal of their fresh appearance. And while pizza dough can be left to rise in the refrigerator for up to 24 hours, the pizzas themselves are at their best straight from the oven.

In addition to bread-based snacks, this chapter offers a few other substantial dishes — such as baked oysters *(page 120)* — that are ideal as a sustaining snack for family or friends.

Cucumber Sandwiches

Makes 48 sandwiches
Working time: about 30 minutes
Total time: about 50 minutes (includes chilling)

Per sandwich:	1	cucumber	1
Calories **25**	¼ tsp	salt	¼ tsp
Protein **trace**			
Cholesterol **5mg**	60 g	unsalted butter, softened	2 oz
Total fat **1g**	2 tbsp	finely cut fresh dill, or	2 tbsp
Saturated fat **trace**		1 ½ tsp dried dill	
Sodium **35mg**		freshly ground black pepper	
	12	thin slices white bread	12

Using a potato peeler, remove the skin from the cucumber. Cut the cucumber into thin slices. Put the slices into a large bowl and sprinkle them with the salt.

Cover the bowl and refrigerate the cucumber slices for at least 30 minutes — the salt will draw out excess moisture from the cucumber and make it crisp.

Meanwhile, put the butter into a bowl with the dill and some black pepper. Beat well together. Arrange the slices of bread on the work surface, in matching pairs, and spread each one thinly with the dill butter.

Drain the cucumber slices in a colander, then pat them dry on paper towels. Arrange the cucumber slices neatly on six of the bread slices, then sandwich together with the remaining slices. Press the sandwiches firmly together. Carefully remove the crusts and cut each sandwich into four squares, then cut each square in half diagonally to make two triangles. Arrange the sandwiches neatly on a serving plate.

Salmon and Watercress Rolls

Makes 36 rolls
Working time: about 40 minutes
Total time: about 2 hours and 50 minutes
(includes cooling and chilling)

Per roll:			
Calories **50**	350 g	salmon steaks	12 oz
Protein **5g**	1	bay leaf	1
Cholesterol **15mg**	1	thyme sprig	1
Total fat **3g**	1	parsley sprig	1
Saturated fat **1g**	1	slice of lemon	1
Sodium **60mg**	8	black peppercorns	8
	¼ tsp	salt	¼ tsp
	2 tbsp	soured cream	2 tbsp
	1 tsp	Dijon mustard	1 tsp
		freshly ground black pepper	
	12	thin slices wholemeal bread	12
	125 g	watercress, stemmed, washed and dried	4 oz
	60 g	unsalted butter, softened	2 oz

Rinse the salmon steaks under cold running water. Place them in a shallow saucepan with the bay leaf, thyme, parsley, lemon, peppercorns, half of the salt and 2 tablespoons of water. Cover the pan with a tightly fitting lid and simmer gently over medium heat until the salmon flakes easily — 8 to 10 minutes. Remove the saucepan from the heat and allow the salmon to cool in the liquid for about 1 hour.

When the salmon is quite cold, carefully remove the skin and bones. Flake the flesh and put it into a bowl. Add the soured cream, mustard, the remaining salt and some pepper, and mix gently together.

Remove the crusts from the slices of bread. Roll each slice with a rolling pin to compress the bread slightly and make it pliable.

Chop the watercress finely, then put it into a small bowl with the butter and beat well together. Spread each slice of bread thinly with the watercress butter. Divide the salmon mixture equally among the slices of bread, then spread evenly over each slice. Neatly roll up the slices of bread, like Swiss rolls, to enclose the salmon. Wrap each roll individually in plastic film to prevent drying, and refrigerate for about 1 hour. Just before serving, remove the plastic film and cut each salmon roll into three.

Party Pinwheels

Makes 240 pinwheels
Working time: about 1 hour and 40 minutes
Total time: about 4 hours (includes chilling)

Per prawn
pinwheel:
Calories **50**
Protein **4g**
Cholesterol **25mg**
Total fat **1g**
Saturated fat **trace**
Sodium **115mg**

Per watercress
pinwheel:
Calories **65**
Protein **3g**
Cholesterol **trace**
Total fat **4g**
Saturated fat **1g**
Sodium **155mg**

Per mushroom
pinwheel:
Calories **60**
Protein **2g**
Cholesterol **trace**
Total fat **3g**
Saturated fat **1g**
Sodium **75mg**

1	small day-old white tin loaf	1
1	small day-old wholemeal tin loaf	1
1	small day-old black rye tin loaf	1
Prawn filling		
350 g	cooked shelled prawns	12 oz
1 tbsp	creamed horseradish	1 tbsp
¼ tsp	white pepper	¼ tsp
1 tbsp	tomato paste	1 tbsp
1 tsp	grated lemon rind	1 tsp
2 tbsp	soured cream or fromage frais	2 tbsp
Watercress filling		
250 g	watercress, washed, thick stems trimmed	8 oz
250 g	medium-fat curd cheese	8 oz
¼ tsp	grated nutmeg	¼ tsp
¼ tsp	salt	¼ tsp
	freshly ground green peppercorns (optional)	
Mushroom filling		
350 g	button mushrooms, wiped clean and finely chopped	12 oz
1 tbsp	Madeira or cognac	1 tbsp
1 tbsp	Dijon mustard	1 tbsp
¼ tsp	salt	¼ tsp
175 g	medium-fat curd cheese	6 oz
½ tsp	ground coriander	½ tsp

To make the prawn filling, blend all the ingredients in a food processor to produce a dense but very smooth purée. Chill while you make the other fillings.

To make the watercress filling, plunge the watercress into lightly boiling water for a few seconds, until bright green and slightly limp. Rinse immediately under cold running water, drain and squeeze hard. In a food processor, blend the watercress together with the curd cheese, nutmeg, salt and some freshly ground green pepper, if using, to form a speckled green purée. Chill the purée in the refrigerator.

To make the mushroom filling, put the mushrooms in a sauté pan with the Madeira or cognac, the mustard and salt. Cover the pan and cook over low heat until the mushrooms are cooked through — about 10 minutes. Remove the lid and continue to cook the mushrooms to evaporate any excess liquid, then cool the mixture. Place the cooked mushrooms in a food processor with the curd cheese and coriander, and process to form a smooth, light brown purée. Chill the purée for about 30 minutes.

Meanwhile, slice each loaf horizontally to give eight slices about 1 cm (½ inch) thick. Trim off the crusts and flatten each slice with a rolling pin to make it more flexible. Cover the bread with plastic film or a clean, damp cloth until you are ready to use it.

Spread one eighth of the prawn mixture on each slice of white bread, one eighth of the watercress purée on each slice of wholemeal bread and one eighth of the mushroom mixture on each slice of rye bread. Make sure that the filling extends to the edges of the bread. Roll up each slice, starting with a shorter side, to make a tight roll, but taking care not to press out any filling. Wrap the rolls in plastic film and chill them for about 2 hours in the refrigerator.

Unwrap the rolls and use a sharp, serrated knife to slice each one into 10 to 12 thin slices; you may need to discard the first and last slices if ragged. Arrange the pinwheels decoratively on a plate to serve.

Seafood Sandwich Gateau

Serves 12
Working time: about 2 hours
Total time: about 4 hours (includes chilling)

Calories **275**			
Protein **17g**	300 g	fresh salmon	10 oz
Cholesterol **50mg**	1	bay leaf	1
Total fat **14g**	1	parsley sprig	1
Saturated fat **3g**	½	small onion	½
Sodium **485mg**	8	black peppercorns	8
	350 g	Dover or lemon sole fillets, skinned	12 oz
	30 cl	unsalted fish stock (recipe, page 139)	½ pint
	15 g	unsalted butter	½ oz
	15 g	plain flour	½ oz
	8 tbsp	chopped parsley	8 tbsp
	7 tbsp	crème fraîche	7 tbsp
	1 tbsp	finely cut fresh dill	1 tbsp
	½ tsp	salt	½ tsp
		freshly ground black pepper	
	175 g	white crab meat, picked over	6 oz
	1	large day-old wholemeal tin loaf	1
	90 g	polyunsaturated margarine	3 oz
		lettuce leaves, washed, dried and shredded	
		radicchio, washed, dried and shredded	
	125 g	medium-fat curd cheese	4 oz
	1	garlic clove, crushed	1

Put the salmon into a saucepan, cover with cold water and add the bay leaf, parsley sprig, onion and peppercorns. Cover the pan and bring just to the boil. Reduce the heat and simmer for 5 minutes. Remove the pan from the heat and let the salmon cool in the water.

Put the sole fillets into a shallow saucepan and cover with the fish stock. Cook gently for 5 to 6 minutes, until the flesh flakes easily. Transfer the fillets to a plate and flake the flesh. Boil the fish stock until it is reduced to 15 cl (¼ pint), then strain through a sieve into a bowl. Melt the butter in the cooking pan and stir in the flour. Gradually stir in the reduced stock. Bring to the boil, stirring all the time, then reduce the heat and simmer gently for 2 to 3 minutes, stirring frequently. Remove from the heat. Stir the flaked sole and 2 tablespoons of the chopped parsley into the sauce. Pour the mixture into a bowl, and cover the surface closely with plastic film to prevent a skin from forming. Allow to cool, then refrigerate until completely cold.

Remove the skin and bones from the salmon. Flake the flesh and put it into a small bowl. Add 2 tablespoons of the *crème fraîche*, the dill, a little of the salt, and some pepper. Mix gently together, cover and set aside. Put the crab meat into a bowl with 1 tablespoon of *crème fraîche*, the remaining salt and some pepper. Mix together, cover and set aside.

Cut the bottom crust from the bread. Cutting horizontally, cut six 5 mm (¼ inch) thick slices from the ▶

loaf. Stack the slices and remove the crusts to form a neat oblong about 20 by 10 cm (8 by 4 inches). Lift the top five slices of bread together; invert the pile and place it next to the bottom slice.

Spread the bottom slice of bread with a thin layer of margarine, then spread the crab mixture evenly on top. Spread the slice on top of the pile very thinly with margarine, then place it margarine side down on the crab meat. Spread the top side with margarine.

Arrange shredded lettuce over this next slice. Spread the next slice on the pile with margarine and place it margarine side down on the lettuce. Spread with margarine, and then with the salmon mixture.

Spread the next slice on the pile of bread with margarine and place it margarine side down on the salmon mixture. Spread with margarine and cover with an even layer of shredded radicchio.

Spread the next slice of bread with margarine and place it margarine side down on the radicchio. Spread with margarine, then with the sole mixture. Spread the remaining slice of bread with margarine and place it margarine side down on the sole.

Press the layers firmly together, then wrap tightly in plastic film. Refrigerate for 1 hour.

To make a coating, beat the curd cheese with the remaining *crème fraîche* and the garlic until smooth and creamy. Unwrap the chilled loaf and place it on a flat serving board. Spread the cheese mixture evenly and smoothly over the loaf, coating it completely.

Sprinkle the loaf liberally with the remaining chopped parsley, pressing it gently into the cheese coating. Refrigerate for about 1 hour before serving.

Chicken and Asparagus Sandwich Gateau

Serves 12
Working time: about 1 hour and 30 minutes
Total time: about 4 hours and 45 minutes (includes chilling)

Calories **180**
Protein **10g**
Cholesterol **30mg**
Total fat **9g**
Saturated fat **3g**
Sodium **250mg**

350 g	skinned and boned chicken breast fillets	12 oz
30 cl	unsalted chicken stock (recipe, page 139)	½ pint
60 g	unsalted butter, softened	2 oz
15 g	plain flour	½ oz
250 g	asparagus spears, trimmed and peeled	8 oz
30 g	polyunsaturated margarine	1 oz
2 tbsp	chopped fresh marjoram, or 2 tsp dried marjoram	2 tbsp
¼ tsp	salt	¼ tsp
	freshly ground black pepper	
1	day-old large white tin loaf	1
½	small head of lettuce, leaves washed, dried and shredded	½
1 tbsp	finely shredded basil leaves	1 tbsp
1 tsp	paprika	1 tsp
Curd cheese coating		
125 g	medium-fat curd cheese	4 oz
60 g	crème fraîche	2 oz
1	garlic clove, crushed	1
2 tsp	mixed fresh chopped herbs or 1 tsp mixed dried herbs	2 tsp

Put the chicken into a saucepan with the stock, cover and cook gently until just tender — 10 to 15 minutes. Allow the chicken to cool in the stock.

Remove the chicken from the stock and chop it finely. Bring the stock to the boil and boil gently until it is reduced to 15 cl (¼ pint). Blend 15 g (½ oz) of the butter with the flour in a small bowl, then gradually whisk into the hot stock. Bring to the boil, stirring until thickened. Reduce the heat and simmer for 2 to 3 minutes. Stir the chicken into the sauce. Pour the sauce into a bowl and cover the surface closely with plastic film to prevent a skin from forming. Cool a little, then refrigerate until completely cold — about 1 hour.

Meanwhile, cook the asparagus spears in boiling water until they are tender — 4 to 6 minutes. Drain the spears in a colander, refresh them under cold running water and drain again well. Put the remaining butter into a bowl with the margarine, marjoram, salt and some pepper. Beat well together.

Remove the bottom crust from the bread. Cutting horizontally, cut five thick slices from the loaf. Stack the slices and remove the crusts to form a neat oblong about 20 by 10 cm (8 by 4 inches). Lift off the top four slices together, and place them upside down next to the bottom slice.

Spread the bottom slice of bread thinly with the marjoram butter, then spread with half of the cold chicken mixture. Spread the slice of bread on top of the pile with butter and place it buttered side down on top of the chicken mixture. Butter again, then arrange the asparagus spears neatly on top. (If the spears are large, slice them in half lengthwise.)

Butter the third slice and place it buttered side down on top of the asparagus. Butter again, then cover with the lettuce and basil. Butter the fourth slice and place it buttered side down on top of the lettuce. Spread with butter and then with the remaining chicken mixture. Spread the remaining slice with butter and place it buttered side down on top of the chicken mixture. Press the layers firmly together, then wrap tightly in plastic film. Refrigerate for 1 hour.

To make the coating, put the curd cheese, *crème fraîche*, garlic and herbs in a bowl and beat well together. Unwrap the chilled loaf and place it on a flat serving board. Spread the cheese mixture evenly and smoothly over the loaf to coat it completely.

Cut strips of greaseproof paper about 1 cm (½ inch) wide and place them diagonally across the top of the loaf. Sprinkle liberally with paprika, then remove the paper strips to leave alternating bands of red and white. Chill the loaf for 1 hour before slicing.

Chicken and Fig on Wholemeal Bread

Serves 4
Working (and total) time: about 10 minutes

Calories **130**
Protein **13g**
Cholesterol **40mg**
Total fat **5g**
Saturated fat **2g**
Sodium **120mg**

15 g	unsalted butter, softened	½ oz
4	slices wholemeal bread	4
2 tsp	cranberry sauce	2 tsp
8	red oakleaf lettuce leaves, washed and dried	8
175 g	cooked chicken breast, thinly sliced	6 oz
2	fresh figs, sliced	2

Butter the bread slices evenly, then spread each slice with ½ teaspoon of the cranberry sauce.

Place two leaves of lettuce on each piece of bread and arrange the chicken breast and fig slices on top.

Roast Beef and Radicchio on Rye Bread

Serves 4
Working (and total) time: about 25 minutes

Calories **195**
Protein **13g**
Cholesterol **40mg**
Total fat **10g**
Saturated fat **4g**
Sodium **60mg**

175 g	new potatoes	6 oz
15 g	unsalted butter, softened	½ oz
4	thin slices dark rye bread	4
12	radicchio leaves, washed and dried	12
175 g	rare roast beef, trimmed of fat and thinly sliced	6 oz
Mustard dressing		
2 tsp	walnut oil	2 tsp
1 tsp	red wine vinegar	1 tsp
⅛ tsp	sugar	⅛ tsp
1 tsp	grainy mustard	1 tsp
	freshly ground black pepper	

Scrub the potatoes and cook them in boiling water until they are cooked but still show resistance when pierced with the tip of a knife — about 10 minutes. Drain them well and leave to cool.

While the potatoes are cooking, mix all the dressing ingredients together in a small bowl and set aside. Spread the butter thinly on the bread and arrange three radicchio leaves on each slice.

Slice the potatoes and divide them among the open sandwiches. Fold the slices of beef and arrange them on top of the potatoes. Spoon a little dressing over each open sandwich and serve.

Tomato and Prosciutto Toasts

Serves 8
Working (and total) time: 20 minutes

Calories **270**
Protein **11g**
Cholesterol **5mg**
Total fat **7g**
Saturated fat **1g**
Sodium **200mg**

4	long crusty bread rolls	4
2	tomatoes, skinned (page 76) and finely chopped	2
2	garlic cloves, crushed	2
2 tbsp	virgin olive oil	2 tbsp
1 tsp	chopped fresh marjoram	1 tsp
¼ tsp	salt	¼ tsp
	freshly ground black pepper	
100 g	thinly sliced prosciutto, trimmed of fat	3½ oz

Cut the rolls in half and toast them on the cut side.

Mix together the chopped tomatoes, garlic, olive oil, marjoram, salt and some freshly ground black pepper. Divide the tomato mixture among the toasted rolls, spread it evenly and press well into the surface.

Cut the prosciutto into strips and arrange a few strips over the top of each roll.

Serve the tomato and prosciutto toasts immediately, while the bread is still warm.

Provençal Sandwich

Serves 4
Working time: about 10 minutes
Total time: about 30 minutes

Calories **305**
Protein **10g**
Cholesterol **0mg**
Total fat **15g**
Saturated fat **2g**
Sodium **595mg**

4	tomatoes	4
2	garlic cloves, crushed	2
3 tbsp	virgin olive oil	3 tbsp
	freshly ground black pepper	
1	baguette (about 60 cm/2 feet long), or four large crusty rolls	1
1	small onion, thinly sliced	1
1	sweet green pepper, cut into rings	1
4	lettuce leaves	4
50 g	canned anchovies, soaked in milk for 20 minutes, drained, rinsed and patted dry	1¾ oz

Skin *(page 76)* and finely chop one tomato. Mix the chopped tomato with the garlic, oil and some pepper.

Split the baguette along one side, without cutting right through the crust. Open it out so that it lies flat, and spread the tomato mixture evenly over the bread.

Slice the remaining tomatoes and place on one half of the baguette, together with the onion and pepper rings. Arrange the lettuce leaves and anchovies on top, and cover with the other half of the baguette.

Press down with your hands, to compress the sandwich and allow the flavours to blend. Cut the baguette diagonally into four pieces, and serve.

Baguette with Hot Prawn and Garlic Filling

Serves 6
Working time: about 10 minutes
Total time: about 20 minutes

Calories **165**	90 g	medium-fat curd cheese	3 oz
Protein **10g**	½	garlic clove, crushed	½
Cholesterol **40mg**	2 tsp	finely chopped fresh herbs such as parsley, chives and dill	2 tsp
Total fat **5g**			
Saturated fat **trace**	1 tsp	fresh lemon juice	1 tsp
Sodium **340mg**		freshly ground black pepper	
	175 g	cooked peeled prawns, chopped	6 oz
	1	baguette, about 60 cm (2 feet) long, or six crusty rolls	1

Preheat the oven to 220°C (425°F or Mark 7).

In a medium-sized bowl, mix together the curd cheese, garlic, herbs, lemon juice and some black pepper. Stir in the prawns.

Cut deep diagonal slashes at 4 cm (1½ inch) intervals in the baguette, taking care not to slice right through. Stuff the slashes with the prawn mixture.

Wrap the baguette loosely in aluminium foil and bake in the oven for 10 minutes. Serve hot.

Savoury Filled Loaf

Serves 6
Working time: about 25 minutes
Total time: about 1 hour

Calories **80**
Protein **4g**
Cholesterol **5mg**
Total fat **3g**
Saturated fat **1g**
Sodium **350mg**

175 g	button mushrooms, wiped clean and quartered or halved	6 oz
1 tbsp	safflower oil	1 tbsp
1 ½ tbsp	fresh lemon juice	1 ½ tbsp
2 tsp	fresh thyme, or ½ tsp dried thyme	2 tsp
½ tsp	salt	½ tsp
	freshly ground black pepper	
1	small white cob loaf, about 15 cm (6 inches) in diameter	1
60 g	thinly sliced prosciutto	2 oz
3	tomatoes, skinned, seeded (page 76) and thinly sliced	3

In a small, heavy frying pan, sauté the mushrooms in the oil and lemon juice until their juices run. Stir in the thyme, salt and a little pepper, then set aside. Preheat the oven to 190°C (375°F or Mark 5).

Slice off the top of the loaf to form a lid about 2.5 cm (1 inch) thick at its centre. With your fingers, scoop out bread from the centre of the loaf, leaving a 1 cm (½ inch) thick base and sides; use the scooped-out bread to make breadcrumbs for another dish.

Arrange the mushrooms in the bottom of the bread-case. Lay the slices of prosciutto on top of the mushrooms; the ends of the slices should overhang the sides of the loaf. Arrange the tomatoes on top of the ham, add a little pepper, then fold over the over-hanging ham to enclose the tomatoes. Replace the lid. Wrap the loaf in foil and bake for 30 minutes. Unwrap the loaf and cut it into wedges. Serve warm.

Beef Salad Tortilla Cones

Makes 8 cones
Working time: about 45 minutes
Total time: about 1 hour and 10 minutes

Per cone:
Calories **280**
Protein **9g**
Cholesterol **15mg**
Total fat **16g**
Saturated fat **4g**
Sodium **195mg**

200 g	plain flour	7 oz
½ tsp	salt	½ tsp
45 g	hard white vegetable fat	1½ oz
175 g	lean beef fillet, cut into 2.5 by 1 cm (1 by ½ inch) pieces	6 oz
½ tbsp	virgin olive oil	½ tbsp
½	crisp lettuce, leaves washed, dried and shredded	½
¼	sweet green pepper, seeded, deribbed and chopped	¼
¼	sweet red pepper, seeded, deribbed and chopped	¼
¼	sweet yellow pepper, seeded, deribbed and chopped	¼
¼	cucumber, halved lengthwise and sliced	¼
2	spring onions, sliced	2
5	black olives, stoned and sliced	5
3	tomatoes, cut into thin wedges	3
Chili and lime marinade		
1	green chili pepper, finely chopped (caution, page 18)	1
1	lime, juice strained and rind grated	1
1	garlic clove, finely chopped	1
½ tbsp	virgin olive oil	½ tbsp
	freshly ground black pepper	

Chili and lime vinaigrette		
1	green chili pepper, finely chopped (caution, page 18)	1
1½ tbsp	fresh lime juice	1½ tbsp
½ tsp	tomato paste	½ tsp
½ tbsp	red wine vinegar	½ tbsp
3 tbsp	virgin olive oil	3 tbsp
1 tsp	finely chopped fresh oregano, or ½ tsp dried oregano	1 tsp
¼ tsp	salt	¼ tsp
	freshly ground black pepper	

First make the tortillas. Mix the flour with the salt and rub in the vegetable fat. Gradually add about 8 cl (3 fl oz) of warm water and knead into a dough for about 1 minute. Add a little more flour if the dough is sticky, or water if it is too dry. Let the dough rest for 15 to 20 minutes, then divide it into four and roll out each piece on a floured worktop to make a 25 cm (10 inch) circle, about 3 mm (⅛ inch) thick. Heat a lightly oiled crêpe or frying pan and fry each tortilla until bubbles form and the surface is slightly speckled — about 30 seconds. Flatten the bubbles with a wooden spatula, then turn the tortilla over and cook for another 30 seconds. Set the cooked tortillas aside.

Preheat the oven to 180°C (350°F or Mark 4).

Mix the ingredients for the marinade together in a shallow bowl. Add the beef, turn the pieces to coat them, and leave to marinate for 15 to 20 minutes.

Prepare the vinaigrette by mixing together the chili

pepper, lime juice, tomato paste, vinegar, oil, oregano, salt and some pepper in a small bowl. Set aside.

Heat the oil in a non-stick frying pan over medium heat. Drain the meat, discarding the marinade, and sauté it for 2 to 3 minutes. Meanwhile, place the tortillas in the oven for 2 to 3 minutes to heat them through; they will dry out if left any longer.

Remove the meat from the pan and mix it in a bowl with the lettuce, sweet peppers, cucumber, spring onions, olives and tomatoes; pour in the vinaigrette and toss. Cut the hot tortillas in half. Fold each tortilla half into a cornet shape and fill it with some of the beef and salad mixture. Serve immediately, while the tortillas and beef are still warm.

Chicken and Orange Pittas

Serves 6
Working (and total) time: about 15 minutes

Calories **180**
Protein **18g**
Cholesterol **5mg**
Total fat **7g**
Saturated fat **1g**
Sodium **230mg**

2	oranges	2
350 g	cooked chicken breast, diced	12 oz
½	small crisp lettuce, leaves washed, dried and torn into bite-sized pieces	½
3	wholemeal pittas	3
	Watercress dressing	
90 g	watercress, washed and dried, thick stems removed	3 oz
2 tbsp	mayonnaise	2 tbsp
2 tbsp	plain low-fat yogurt	2 tbsp
¼ tsp	salt	¼ tsp
	freshly ground black pepper	

Preheat the oven to 200°C (400°F or Mark 6). Put all the ingredients for the dressing in a blender or food processor and purée for a few seconds until smooth. Set the dressing aside.

Cut away the peel, white pith and outer membrane from the oranges. To separate the orange segments from the inner membranes, slice down to the core with a sharp knife on either side of each segment; cut each segment in half. Place the chicken, lettuce and orange segments in a bowl and mix together.

Warm the pittas in the oven until they puff up — about 1 minute. Cut them in half, then open up each half to form a pocket; stuff the pittas with the chicken mixture. Spoon generous amounts of watercress dressing into each pitta half and serve immediately.

Creamed Mushrooms on Toast

Serves 2
Working (and total) time: about 15 minutes

Calories **150**
Protein **5g**
Cholesterol **10mg**
Total fat **5g**
Saturated fat **2g**
Sodium **400mg**

2	slices granary bread	2
15 cl	unsalted chicken or vegetable stock (recipes, page 139)	¼ pint
1 tbsp	Madeira	1 tbsp
1 tsp	fresh lemon juice	1 tsp
175 g	button mushrooms, wiped clean	6 oz
2 tbsp	crème fraîche	2 tbsp
¼ tsp	salt	¼ tsp
	freshly ground black pepper	
½ tsp	Dijon mustard	½ tsp
½ tsp	mustard seeds	½ tsp

Toast the bread slices on one side only and set aside.

Pour the stock, Madeira and lemon juice into a shallow, lidded saucepan and bring to the boil. Reduce the heat, add the mushrooms and simmer them for about 4 minutes. With a slotted spoon, remove the mushrooms and set them aside.

To reduce the cooking liquid, place the saucepan over high heat and boil until about 2 tablespoons of liquid remain. Add the *crème fraîche* and reduce further for a few seconds. Return the mushrooms to the liquid, warm through, and season with the salt, some pepper and the mustard.

Pour the mixture on to the untoasted side of the bread, sprinkle with the mustard seeds and place under a hot grill for about 20 seconds, until the seeds "pop". Serve at once.

Seafood and Asparagus Muffins

Serves 4
Working (and total) time: about 30 minutes

Calories **180**
Protein **15g**
Cholesterol **50mg**
Total fat **8g**
Saturated fat **4g**
Sodium **365mg**

4	asparagus spears, trimmed and peeled	4
16	fresh mussels, scrubbed and debearded	16
30 g	unsalted butter, softened	1 oz
2 tsp	tomato paste	2 tsp
1 tbsp	finely chopped fresh dill	1 tbsp
2	wholemeal muffins or baps	2
125 g	peeled, cooked prawns	4 oz

Cook the asparagus in a saucepan of boiling water until tender — 5 to 6 minutes — then drain in a colander and refresh under cold running water. Drain well. Cut off the tips, leaving them whole, and slice the stalks. Set the asparagus aside.

Pour 4 tablespoons of water into a large saucepan. Add the mussels, cover the pan and bring the water to the boil. Steam the mussels until their shells open — 4 to 5 minutes. Let the mussels cool in their liquid, then remove them from the pan, discarding any that remain closed. Using your fingers or the edge of a spoon, detach the flesh from the shells. Set the mussels aside and discard the shells.

In a small bowl, mix together the butter, tomato paste and dill, blending them well. Split the muffins in half and toast them under a hot grill for 1 to 2 minutes each side until they are lightly browned.

Spread the muffin halves thinly with about half of the tomato butter, then divide the mussels, prawns, and asparagus slices and tips among the muffins. Melt the remaining tomato butter and brush it over the top of the seafood and asparagus.

Place the muffins under a medium grill for 3 to 4 minutes, to heat them through, and serve immediately.

Baked Oysters

Makes 12 oysters
Working time: about 30 minutes
Total time: about 40 minutes

Per oyster:
Calories **45**
Protein **5g**
Cholesterol **20mg**
Total fat **2g**
Saturated fat **1g**
Sodium **190mg**

350 g	spinach, washed and stemmed	12 oz
15 g	unsalted butter	½ oz
6	spring onions, trimmed and finely sliced	6
	freshly ground black pepper	
12	fresh oysters	12
	coarse salt for baking	
Parmesan topping		
30 g	Parmesan cheese, finely grated	1 oz
15 g	fresh wholemeal breadcrumbs	½ oz
1 tbsp	finely chopped parsley	1 tbsp

Preheat the oven to 220°C (425°F or Mark 7).

Plunge the spinach into a saucepan of boiling water, and boil for 30 seconds. Drain the spinach in a colander and refresh it under cold running water. Squeeze the spinach dry, then chop it finely.

Heat the butter in a frying pan then add the spring onions and cook them gently until they are softened — 2 to 3 minutes. Stir in the spinach and cook for 3 to 4 minutes, stirring frequently. Season with some black pepper.

Mix the topping ingredients together. Open the oysters *(below)* and discard their flat half shells. With the oysters on their rounder half shells, divide the spinach mixture equally among them, spooning it neatly on top. Sprinkle the Parmesan topping evenly over the oysters.

Pour coarse salt into a large ovenproof dish to a depth of about 2.5 cm (1 inch). Place the oysters on the bed of salt and bake in the oven for 10 to 15 minutes, until they are golden-brown. Serve warm.

Shucking an Oyster

1 *OPENING THE SHELLS. Scrub the oyster well. Place it on a work surface with its rounder side down to catch the liquid. Grip the oyster with a towel to protect your hand, leaving the hinged end exposed, and force the tip of an oyster knife or other broad blade into the hinge. Twist the blade to prise the shells apart.*

2 *FREEING THE OYSTER. Sliding the knife blade along the inside of the upper shell, sever the muscle that attaches the flesh to the shell. Discard the upper shell, then slide the blade under the oyster and cut it free.*

Goat Cheese on Toast

Serves 4
Working time: about 30 minutes
Total time: about 12 hours and 40 minutes
(includes marinating)

Calories **180**
Protein **8g**
Cholesterol **20mg**
Total fat **11g**
Saturated fat **4g**
Sodium **370mg**

2	small goat cheeses, about 100 g (3½ oz) total weight	2
2 tbsp	virgin olive oil	2 tbsp
½ tsp	crushed black peppercorns	½ tsp
1	bay leaf	1
1	garlic clove, crushed	1
1 tbsp	finely chopped fresh herbs, such as chives, tarragon or rosemary	1 tbsp
4	thin slices French bread, cut diagonally	4
30 g	fresh breadcrumbs	1 oz
125 g	assorted salad leaves	4 oz

Remove the thin layer of rind on the cheeses and cut each cheese into four rounds. Mix the oil, peppercorns, bay leaf, garlic and herbs in a bowl, and add the cheese rounds. Turn them so that they are well coated, then leave them to marinate in the refrigerator for about 12 hours.

Preheat the oven to 180°C (350°F or Mark 4). Put the bread slices in the oven for about 4 minutes, then brush them with the marinade. Meanwhile, increase the temperature to 240°C (475°F or Mark 9).

Remove the cheese slices from the marinade and dip them in the breadcrumbs, pressing lightly to make the crumbs adhere. Place two cheese slices on each toast and return to the oven until the toast is slightly brown and the cheese softened — about 10 minutes. Serve the hot toasts surrounded by the salad leaves.

EDITOR'S NOTE: *The marinade may be reserved and used to dress the salad leaves, but this will increase the calorie and fat content of the snack.*

Tuna Tapenade Pizzas

IN THIS RECIPE TUNA FISH REPLACES A LARGE PERCENTAGE
OF THE OILY INGREDIENTS OF THE TRADITIONAL PROVENÇAL
TAPENADE — AN OIL, OLIVE AND ANCHOVY PURÉE.

Serves 6
Working time: about 40 minutes
Total time: about 2 hours (includes proving)

Calories **340**
Protein **14g**
Cholesterol **25mg**
Total fat **15g**
Saturated fat **2g**
Sodium **305mg**

15 g	fresh yeast, or 7 g (¼ oz) dried yeast	½ oz
300 g	plain flour	10 oz
1 tsp	salt	1 tsp
1 tbsp	virgin olive oil	1 tbsp
6	cherry tomatoes, sliced, for garnish	6
	chopped parsley, for garnish (optional)	
	Tuna tapenade	
3	anchovy fillets, rinsed, dried and finely chopped	3
1	garlic clove, finely chopped	1
1½ tbsp	capers, finely chopped	1½ tbsp
12	black olives, stoned and finely chopped	12
200 g	tuna fish canned in brine, drained	7 oz
1 tbsp	virgin olive oil	1 tbsp
	freshly ground black pepper	

Mix the fresh yeast with 15 cl (¼ pint) of tepid water
and leave it to activate for 10 to 15 minutes; if you are
using dried yeast, reconstitute according to the
manufacturer's instructions. Sift the flour and salt into
a large bowl and make a well in the flour. When the
yeast solution is frothy, pour it into the well along with
the oil and mix in enough tepid water to make a soft
but firm dough. On a floured work surface, knead the
dough until it is smooth and elastic — about 10
minutes — then gather the dough into a ball and leave
it in a clean bowl, covered with plastic film, until it has
doubled in size — about 1 hour.

Preheat the oven to 220°C (425°F or Mark 7) and
lightly oil a baking tray. Knock the dough back, then
divide it into six balls. On a floured work surface, roll
out each ball into a 12 cm (5 inch) diameter circle.
Press the edges of the circles to create a raised rim.
Put the circles on the prepared baking tray and leave
to rise a little — at least 10 minutes.

For the tapenade, pound the anchovies and garlic
together in a mortar. Add the capers, olives, tuna fish,
oil and some pepper in gradual stages, continuing to
pound to form a paste. Divide the paste equally among
the pizza bases and spread it to within 5 mm (¼ inch)
of the edges. Bake for 15 minutes, then garnish with
the tomato slices and return to the oven for 5 minutes.
Serve warm, garnished, if you like, with parsley.

Calzone

THE DOUGH AND INGREDIENTS OF CALZONE ARE VERY SIMILAR
TO THOSE OF PIZZA; INSTEAD OF AN OPEN FLAN, THE DOUGH IS
FOLDED OVER TO ENVELOPE THE FILLING. THE SHAPE OF
CALZONE DIFFERS FROM ONE REGION OF ITALY TO ANOTHER —
CRESCENTS, SQUARES AND TRIANGLES ARE ALL TO BE FOUND.

Makes 10 calzone
Working time: about 40 minutes
Total time: about 2 hours (includes proving)

Per calzone:
Calories **225**
Protein **11g**
Cholesterol **15mg**
Total fat **6g**
Saturated fat **3g**
Sodium **400mg**

500 g	plain flour, sifted	· 1 lb
1 ½ tsp	salt	1 ½ tsp
15 g	fresh yeast, or 7 g (¼ oz) dried yeast	½ oz
1 tbsp	virgin olive oil	1 tbsp
500 g	large tomatoes, skinned (page 76) and chopped	1 lb
1 tbsp	tomato paste	1 tbsp
1 tsp	dried oregano	1 tsp
	freshly ground black pepper	
175 g	low-fat mozzarella cheese, sliced	6 oz
60 g	prosciutto, chopped	2 oz

Cream the fresh yeast with 15 cl (¼ pint) of tepid water and leave for 10 to 15 minutes, until frothy. If using dried yeast, reconstitute according to the manufacturer's instructions. Sift the flour and salt into a large bowl and make a well in the centre. Pour in the yeast mixture and mix in enough tepid water to make a soft but firm dough. Turn the dough on to a floured surface and knead until it is smooth and elastic — about 10 minutes. Return the dough to the bowl, cover with plastic film and leave to rise in a warm place until doubled in size — about 1 hour.

To make the filling, heat the oil in a small pan over medium heat, add the tomatoes and tomato paste, and cook for about 5 minutes. Stir in the oregano, the remaining salt and some pepper, then leave to cool. Preheat the oven to 220°C (425°F or Mark 7).

Turn the dough on to a floured surface, knead for a few minutes, then divide it into 10 pieces. Roll out each piece into a rectangle approximately 20 by 10 cm (8 by 4 inches). Spread the tomato mixture over one half of each rectangle, leaving a small border; reserve any tomato juices in the pan. Top the tomato mixture with the mozzarella and prosciutto, then dampen the edges of the dough, fold the dough over the filling, and press the edges together to seal them. Arrange the calzone on a lightly oiled baking sheet and brush them with the reserved tomato juices. Cover with plastic film and leave to rise for 10 minutes.

Bake the calzone in the oven until they are puffed up and golden — 8 to 10 minutes. Serve hot.

SUGGESTED ACCOMPANIMENT: *leafy salad.*

Herbed Focaccia

FOCACCIA IS A GENOESE BREAD MADE WITH OLIVE OIL. HERE
HALF OF THE BREAD HAS A TOMATO AND BRESAOLA TOPPING,
WHILE HALF IS SERVED PLAIN.

Serves 12
Working time: about 45 minutes
Total time: about 2 hours and 15 minutes (includes proving)

Calories **260**
Protein **8g**
Cholesterol **5mg**
Total fat **5g**
Saturated fat **1g**
Sodium **125mg**

30 g	fresh yeast, or 15 g (½ oz) dried yeast	1 oz
750 g	strong plain flour	1½ lb
¾ tsp	salt	¾ tsp
3 tbsp	virgin olive oil	3 tbsp
6	leaves fresh sage, finely chopped	6
1 tbsp	finely chopped rosemary leaves	1 tbsp
1 tbsp	chopped fresh oregano or marjoram	1 tbsp
2 tbsp	chopped or torn basil leaves	2 tbsp
30 g	green olives, stoned and finely chopped	1 oz
2 tbsp	chopped rosemary, sage or basil leaves	2 tbsp
2	large tomatoes, thinly sliced	2
30 g	bresaola, cut into strips	1 oz

Blend the fresh yeast with 3 tablespoons of warm water, and leave to activate for 10 to 15 minutes; if you are using dried yeast, reconstitute according to the manufacturer's instructions. Sift the flour with ½ teaspoon of the salt, make a well in the centre, and pour in 2 tablespoons of the olive oil and 35 cl (12 fl oz) of tepid water. Add the sage, rosemary, oregano, basil and olives, then the yeast mixture. Gradually incorporate the flour into the liquid and knead the dough well for about 10 minutes, until it is elastic and no longer sticky. Form the dough into a ball, brush lightly with a little olive oil, place it in a large bowl, cover with plastic film, and leave in a warm place to prove until it has doubled in volume — about 1 hour.

Lightly brush two 30 by 22 cm (12 by 9 inch) baking tins with a little olive oil. Knock back the risen dough and, with floured hands, knead it for a further minute or two on a lightly floured surface. Stretch and press the dough until it is about 2 cm (¾ inch) thick. Divide the dough in half and press it into the prepared tins, pushing it hard into the corners.

Dimple the surface of the dough with your knuckles and brush with the remaining olive oil. Sprinkle one tin of dough with the remaining salt; sprinkle the other with the 2 tablespoons of rosemary, sage or basil, and arrange the tomato slices over the top.

Preheat the oven to 230°C (450°F or Mark 8). Leave the dough to prove for 15 to 25 minutes, until it has almost doubled in size. Bake in the centre of the oven until lightly golden — 15 to 20 minutes. Remove the tomato-garnished focaccia from the oven, scatter the bresaola between the rows of tomato and return to the oven for just 1 minute. Remove both tins from the oven and transfer the focaccia to a wire rack. Cut each into 12 pieces and serve while still warm.

Chicken and Walnut Pizzas

Serves 6
Working time: about 45 minutes
Total time: about 2 hours

Calories **365**
Protein **19g**
Cholesterol **30mg**
Total fat **15g**
Saturated fat **3g**
Sodium **180mg**

3	chicken thighs (about 350 g/12 oz)	3
1	carrot, coarsely chopped	1
1	large onion, coarsely chopped, plus 1 tsp finely chopped onion	1
6	black peppercorns	6
1	thyme sprig	1
1	bay leaf	1
75 g	shelled walnuts	2½ oz
1	garlic clove, finely chopped	1
⅛ tsp	cayenne pepper	⅛ tsp
⅛ tsp	paprika	⅛ tsp
¼ tsp	salt	¼ tsp
½	sweet red pepper, cored, deribbed, seeded and sliced into rings	½
	parsley, for garnish	
Pizza dough		
15 g	fresh yeast, or 7 g (¼ oz) dried yeast	½ oz
300 g	plain flour	10 oz
¼ tsp	salt	¼ tsp
1 tbsp	virgin olive oil	1 tbsp

First, make the pizza dough. Mix the yeast with a little tepid water and leave it for 10 to 15 minutes, until frothy. If using dried yeast, reconstitute according to the manufacturer's instructions. Sift the flour and salt into a large bowl. Pour in the yeast mixture together with the oil and mix in enough tepid water to make a soft but firm dough. On a floured work surface, knead the dough until it is smooth and elastic — about 10 minutes. Form it into a ball, then leave it in a clean bowl, covered, until doubled in size — about 1 hour.

While the dough is proving, put the chicken thighs in a saucepan and pour in cold water to cover them. Add the carrot, coarsely chopped onion, peppercorns, thyme and bay leaf. Bring to the boil, then reduce the heat, cover and simmer gently for 15 to 20 minutes. Take the pan off the heat and leave to cool.

Preheat the oven to 220°C (425°F or Mark 7) and lightly oil two baking sheets. Punch the dough down to deflate it, then divide it into six balls. On a floured work surface, roll out each ball into a 15 by 10 cm (6 by 4 inch) oval. Press up the edges to form raised rims, then put the ovals on the baking sheets and leave them to prove a little more.

Meanwhile, strain the chicken stock into a bowl and reserve it. Skin and bone the chicken thighs and coarsely chop the meat.

In a food processor, finely chop the walnuts, then mix in the finely chopped onion, the garlic, cayenne pepper, paprika and salt. Add up to 15 cl (¼ pint) of the reserved stock to make a smooth, pale sauce when thoroughly blended.

Divide the sauce among the pizza bases and spread it to within 5 mm (¼ inch) of the edges. Bake the pizzas in the oven for 10 to 15 minutes. Sprinkle each one with the chopped chicken and a red pepper ring, then return the pizzas to the oven for another 5 to 10 minutes. Serve warm, garnished with the parsley.

Scallop Galettes

Serves 8
Working time: about 45 minutes
Total time: about 1 hour

Calories **165**
Protein **9g**
Cholesterol **50mg**
Total fat **6g**
Saturated fat **3g**
Sodium **270mg**

100 g	buckwheat flour	3½ oz
45 g	plain flour	1½ oz
¾ tsp	salt	¾ tsp
30 g	unsalted butter	1 oz
1 tsp	clear honey	1 tsp
1	egg, lightly beaten	1
22.5 cl	dry cider	7½ fl oz
500 g	spinach, washed, stems removed	1 lb
45 g	crème fraîche	1½ oz
	freshly ground black pepper	
	grated nutmeg	
¼ tsp	safflower oil	¼ tsp
8	shelled scallops, bright white connective tissue removed, scallops rinsed, corals reserved	8
	freshly ground green peppercorns (optional)	

To make the galette batter, first sift the flours and ¼ teaspoon of the salt into a mixing bowl and form a well in the centre. Melt 15 g (½ oz) of the butter and pour it into the well with ½ teaspoon of the honey, the egg, 15 cl (¼ pint) of the cider and 15 cl (¼ pint) of water. Using a wooden spoon, gradually draw the dry ingredients into the liquids. Beat lightly until free of lumps, then set aside to rest for about 30 minutes.

Place the washed spinach, with water still clinging to the leaves, in a large, heavy-bottomed saucepan. Cover, and steam the spinach over medium heat until wilted — 2 to 3 minutes. Drain the spinach quickly, squeeze out all excess moisture and chop roughly with a knife. Return the spinach to the saucepan and stir in 1 tablespoon of the remaining cider and half the *crème fraîche*. Season with ¼ teaspoon of the salt and some pepper and nutmeg. Set aside until you are ready to serve the galettes.

When the batter is ready, heat an 18 cm (7 inch) crêpe or non-stick frying pan *(page 86)* over medium-high heat. Add the oil and spread it over the entire surface with a paper towel. Put 2 to 3 tablespoons of the batter into the pan, and immediately swirl the pan to coat the bottom with a thin, even layer of batter. Cook until the bottom is lightly browned — about 30 seconds. Lift the edge with a spatula and turn the galette over. Cook it on the second side until that too is lightly browned. Slide the galette on to a heated plate.

Repeat the process with the remaining batter, brushing the pan lightly with more oil if the galettes begin to stick. Stack the cooked galettes on the plate as you go, and then cover with a tea towel and set aside; or keep them warm in a 150°C (300°F or Mark 2) oven until all eight are cooked and ready to fill.

Slice each scallop horizontally into two or three rounds. Finely slice the corals. Melt the remaining butter in a heavy frying pan and toss the scallop slices in the butter until they are no longer opaque — about 2 minutes. Add the remaining cider and the sliced corals, and cook over medium heat for a further 30 seconds. Mix in the rest of the *crème fraîche*, honey and salt, season with some nutmeg and return to the heat for a few seconds to amalgamate. Remove the frying pan from the heat. Reheat the spinach mixture over medium heat, stirring continuously.

To serve, place a spoonful of spinach in the centre of each galette and arrange two or three scallop slices and a sprinkling of coral in each "nest" of spinach. Fold over the four rounded edges of each galette to form a small, square parcel, leaving the scallop slices partly exposed. Sprinkle a little freshly ground green pepper over the top of each scallop filling if you like, and serve immediately.

Spanish Tortilla Triangles

Serves 8
Working time: about 15 minutes
Total time: about 30 minutes

Calories **100**
Protein **4g**
Cholesterol **110mg**
Total fat **7g**
Saturated fat **2g**
Sodium **135mg**

2 tbsp	virgin olive oil	2 tbsp
2	leeks, trimmed, cleaned (below) and cut diagonally into fine slices	2
2	garlic cloves, finely chopped	2
1	sweet red pepper, seeded, deribbed and finely chopped	1
1	sweet green pepper, seeded, deribbed and finely chopped	1
4	eggs	4
½ tsp	salt	½ tsp
	freshly ground black pepper	
250 g	cooked peeled potatoes, chopped	8 oz
2 tbsp	chopped parsley	2 tbsp

Heat 1½ tablespoons of the oil in a heavy frying pan and cook the leeks over low heat until softened — about 10 minutes. Add the garlic and peppers and cook for a further 10 minutes, stirring occasionally.

Mix the eggs in a bowl with the salt and some pepper, then stir in the cooked vegetable mixture, potatoes and parsley. Preheat the grill to high.

Heat the remaining oil in a 22 cm (9 inch) omelette pan and pour in the egg mixture. Cook over low heat for 4 minutes, until the bottom of the omelette is golden-brown — lift gently with a palette knife to check. Place the pan under the grill and cook until the egg is set — about 3 minutes. Slide the omelette on to a plate, cut into eight triangles and serve at once.

Cleaning Leeks

1 *SPLITTING THE LEEK. Remove any bruised outer leaves from the leek. Cut off the root base and the tough leaf tops. With a paring knife, pierce the leek about 5cm (2 inches) below the green portion, then draw the knife through to the top to split the leek.*

2 *RINSING OUT THE GRIT. Dip the leafy part of the leek into a bowl of water and swirl it vigorously to flush out the grit. Alternatively, rinse well under running water. Run your fingers along the insides of the leaves to remove any remaining particles of sand.*

4 *Pitta bread pockets bulging with vegetables (recipe, opposite page) provide a satisfying hot snack rich in minerals and vitamins.*

Snacks from the Microwave

By their very nature, party foods and light snacks often call for speedy production, and it is in preparing them that a microwave oven truly earns its place in the busy kitchen. While retaining the healthful aspects of the preceding chapters, the recipes given here are all designed to capitalize on the microwave's abbreviated process. The dough for a pizza *(page 138)*, for example, can be proved in just 20 minutes instead of the more usual hour, while the jacket potatoes on page 135 take a mere 10 minutes to cook — less than a quarter of the time they would in a conventional oven. And most of the dishes can be prepared in advance, then cooked or reheated rapidly at the last moment.

The microwave oven offers several bonuses in addition to speed. Because they spend a short time in the oven, with little or no added liquid, vegetables cook in their own juices. As a result, few vital nutrients are lost, and the vegetables emerge with all their natural colouring and texture intact. Moreover, food cooked in the microwave does not brown — except with the aid of a special browning dish. While generally unsuitable for traditional roasts and crusty gratins, this can be turned to positive advantage. Low-calorie wrappers such as cabbage leaves *(page 130)* can be substituted for high-fat pastry without the risk of charring, and bread-wrapped dishes such as the ginger stirred vegetables *(page 129)*, can be reheated without their cases drying out as they might in a regular oven.

One note of caution: some of these recipes call for the food to be covered with plastic film, but be sure to use only plastic film labelled as microwave-safe. And if covering a dish containing liquid, make sure to leave a corner of the film open or slit it with a knife, to prevent a dangerous build-up of steam.

All of the recipes have been tested in 625-watt and 700-watt ovens. But, since power settings vary among ovens made by different manufacturers, the term "high" is used here to indicate 100 per cent power, "medium" for 70 per cent, and "low" for 30 per cent. Because it is easy to overcook food in the microwave, always use the shortest time specified.

Ginger-Stirred Vegetables in Pitta

Serves 4
Working (and total) time: about 20 minutes

Calories **165**
Protein **5g**
Cholesterol **0mg**
Total fat **5g**
Saturated fat **1g**
Sodium **390mg**

2	large pittas, or four small pittas	2
1 tbsp	light sesame oil	1 tbsp
1	small garlic clove, crushed	1
2	2.5 cm (1 inch) pieces fresh ginger root, peeled	2
60 g	fresh shiitake mushrooms, sliced, or 30 g (1 oz) dried shiitake mushrooms, soaked, drained and sliced	2 oz
100 g	baby sweetcorn, sliced	3 ½ oz
250 g	courgettes, julienned	8 oz
1 tbsp	fresh lemon juice	1 tbsp
1 tsp	tamari, or 1 tsp shoyu mixed with ½ tsp honey	1 tsp
¼ tsp	salt	¼ tsp
	freshly ground black pepper	

Wrap the pittas in paper towels and microwave on high for 30 seconds. Cut large pittas in half crosswise or, if using small ones, cut them open along one side.

Place the oil and garlic in a wide, shallow dish. Using a garlic press, squeeze the juice from one piece of ginger, and shred the second piece very finely. Add the ginger juice and shreds to the oil.

Microwave the oil and flavourings on high for 30 seconds. Add the mushrooms to the dish, cover with plastic film, leaving a corner open, and microwave on medium for 2 minutes. Add the sweetcorn, re-cover the dish, leaving a corner open as before, and microwave for a further 2 minutes on medium. Then add the courgettes to the mushrooms and sweetcorn and microwave, uncovered, on high for 1 minute. Season with the lemon juice, tamari or shoyu and honey, salt and some freshly ground pepper, and divide the mixture among the pitta pockets.

Arrange the pittas on paper towels or a serving dish in a single layer, evenly spaced. Microwave them on medium for 1½ minutes, rearranging the pittas half way through to ensure even cooking. Serve at once.

Vegetable Tartouillats

Makes 8 tartouillats
Working (and total) time: about 40 minutes

Per tartouillat:
Calories **100**
Protein **7g**
Cholesterol **35mg**
Total fat **5g**
Saturated fat **2g**
Sodium **160mg**

8	small savoy cabbage leaves	8
300 g	courgettes, finely shredded	10 oz
100 g	carrots, peeled and finely grated	3 ½ oz
1 tbsp	fresh lemon juice	1 tbsp
250 g	medium-fat curd cheese	8 oz
1	egg yolk	1
45 g	fromage frais	1 ½ oz
½ tsp	dry mustard	½ tsp
1 tbsp	potato flour	1 tbsp
1 tsp	ground cinnamon	1 tsp
1 tbsp	chopped fresh basil	1 tbsp
15 g	feta cheese, crumbled	½ oz
1 tsp	finely chopped mint, plus eight mint sprigs, for garnish	1 tsp

Blanch the cabbage leaves in a saucepan of boiling, lightly salted water for 3 to 5 minutes, until they are pliable but still firm. Drain them, rinse under cold running water, then dry them thoroughly on absorbent paper towels. Cut away any hard central ribs from the leaves and use each leaf to line a microwave muffin mould or ramekin. Using kitchen scissors, trim round the edges of the cabbage leaves so that they rise no more than 2.5 cm (1 inch) above the rim of the moulds.

Place the shredded courgettes in a shallow dish and cover with plastic film, leaving a corner open to allow the steam to escape. Microwave on high for 3 minutes, stirring twice during this time. Drain in a fine-meshed sieve. Place the grated carrots in the dish with a few drops of the lemon juice, and cover with plastic film, again leaving a corner open. Microwave on high for 2 minutes, then set the dish aside. If the curd cheese is chilled, soften it a little by microwaving on low for about 45 seconds.

In a mixing bowl, beat the curd cheese with the egg yolk until thoroughly blended. In another bowl, mix together the *fromage frais* and remaining lemon juice, blend in the mustard and potato flour, and stir until free of lumps. Add this mixture to the curd cheese and beat gently but thoroughly. Squeeze the drained courgettes to remove any remaining liquid, then add the courgettes, carrots, cinnamon and basil to the cheese mixture. Stir well. Divide the mixture among the eight lined moulds, and sprinkle a little of the feta cheese and chopped mint on top of each.

Arrange the moulds in the microwave oven, making sure they are evenly spaced; a circle of moulds would be ideal. Microwave on medium low for 8 minutes, rearranging the moulds every 2 minutes. Leave to stand for 2 minutes, then check that the centres are fairly firm to the touch. If they are not, cook for a further 2 minutes on low and test again. If necessary, cook the tartlets for a final 2 minutes on low, then remove from the oven; the centres will firm while the tartlets are resting for a minute or two.

Serve the tartlets warm or at room temperature, garnished with the mint sprigs.

Vegetable Purées in Chicory

Makes about 50 leaves
Working time: about 40 minutes
Total time: about 1 hour

Per leaf:			
Calories **60**	300 g	carrots, peeled and roughly sliced	10 oz
Protein **2g**	1	orange, grated rind of half, juice of whole	1
Cholesterol **0mg**			
Total fat **2g**	350 g	Brussels sprouts, trimmed	12 oz
Saturated fat **trace**	350 g	potatoes, scrubbed well, dried and pricked all over with a fork	12 oz
Sodium **90mg**			
	175 g	fromage frais	6 oz
	1 tsp	ground coriander	1 tsp
	¼ tsp	white pepper	¼ tsp
	¾ tsp	salt	¾ tsp
	1 tbsp	hazelnut oil	1 tbsp
	¼ tsp	grated nutmeg	¼ tsp
	1	small bunch flat-leaf parsley, chopped	1
	4	heads chicory	4

Place the carrots, orange rind and juice in a dish. Cover the dish with plastic film, leaving one corner open, and microwave on high until the carrots are just tender — about 8 minutes. Set aside to cool.

Place the sprouts with 4 tablespoons of water in another dish. Cover the dish with plastic film, leaving one corner open, and microwave on high until the sprouts are just soft — 6 to 8 minutes. Leave to cool.

Arrange the potatoes, evenly spaced, on paper towels in the oven. Microwave on high for about 10 minutes, turning them over half way through cooking. Leave to rest for 2 minutes; if they are not then soft, microwave for a further 2 to 5 minutes. Leave to cool, then remove the skins.

In a food processor or blender, process the carrots until finely chopped. Add 45 g (1½ oz) of the *fromage frais*, the coriander, white pepper and ¼ teaspoon of the salt, and blend until puréed.

Remove the carrot purée from the processor and clean the bowl. Process the sprouts until finely chopped, then add the oil, nutmeg and ¼ teaspoon of the salt, and blend again until puréed. Add 30 g (1 oz) of the *fromage frais* and blend to form a very smooth purée. Mash the potatoes, then beat them with the parsley and the remaining *fromage frais* and salt until soft and amalgamated.

Separate the chicory leaves, and wash and dry them carefully. Using a piping bag fitted with a large star nozzle, fill one third of the leaves with the carrot purée, one third with the sprout purée and one third with the potato purée. Arrange on a platter and serve.

Spiced Coconut Crab Dip with Poppadoms

Serves 8
Working (and total) time: about 30 minutes

Calories **140**
Protein **9g**
Cholesterol **30mg**
Total fat **5g**
Saturated fat **1g**
Sodium **260mg**

60 g	creamed coconut	2 oz
¼ litre	unsalted chicken stock (recipe, page 139)	8 fl oz
2.5 cm	piece fresh ginger root, peeled and sliced	1 inch
6	cardamom pods, crushed	6
1	blade mace	1
2	chili peppers, split lengthwise and seeded (caution, page 18)	2
1	fresh turmeric root, sliced, or ½ teaspoon ground turmeric	1
⅛ tsp	saffron threads	⅛ tsp
1	lime or bay leaf	1
5 tbsp	soured cream	5 tbsp
2 tsp	cornflour	2 tsp
1 tsp	dry mustard	1 tsp
2 tbsp	dry sherry	2 tbsp
1 tbsp	tomato paste	1 tbsp
125 g	white crab meat, picked over	4 oz
125 g	brown crab meat, picked over	4 oz
1	tamarillo, peeled, seeded and finely diced	1
1 tsp	fresh lemon juice	1 tsp
½ tsp	salt	½ tsp
¼ tsp	cayenne pepper, plus a sprinkling, for garnish	¼ tsp
16	poppadoms	16
	finely shredded chili pepper, for garnish	

Blend the creamed coconut with the chicken stock in a bowl. Add the ginger, cardamom, mace, chilies, turmeric, saffron and lime or bay leaf. Microwave on low for 5 minutes, to infuse the liquid with the spices. Strain the coconut mixture through a sieve into a 90 cl (1½ pint) dish, pressing down hard on the spices. Stir in the soured cream and mix well.

In a small bowl, blend the cornflour, mustard powder and sherry, and stir this into the coconut mixture. Then stir in the tomato paste. Microwave the mixture on medium for about 3 minutes, or until the liquid has thickened and begun to bubble.

Stir the white and brown crab meat into the coconut-tomato mixture, and microwave for 30 seconds on medium. Stir in the diced tamarillo and microwave for a further 30 seconds, again on medium. Finally, add the lemon juice, salt and cayenne pepper.

Place four poppadoms at a time in the microwave oven in a single layer on paper towels and cook on high for about 1 minute, rearranging after 30 seconds; the poppadoms are cooked when they appear evenly "puffed" and no dark patches remain.

Meanwhile, transfer the dip to a serving dish and garnish with a little shredded chili and a sprinkling of cayenne. Serve at once with the poppadoms.

Spinach and Salmon Canapés

Makes 12 canapés
Working time: about 25 minutes
Total time: about 30 minutes

Per canapé:			
Calories **90**	250 g	salmon steak, skinned and boned	8 oz
Protein **9g**	2	egg whites	2
Cholesterol **25mg**	175 g	skinned sole or plaice fillets	6 oz
Total fat **4g**	2 tbsp	quark	2 tbsp
Saturated fat **1g**	1	small sweet red pepper, pricked all over with a fork	1
Sodium **140mg**	175 g	spinach leaves, stemmed, washed and drained	6 oz
	6	slices wholemeal bread	6

Finely chop the salmon in a food processor, then blend in one egg white. Tip the mixture into a bowl. Repeat this procedure with the sole or plaice and the second egg white. Stir 1 tablespoon of the quark into each of the mixtures and chill them.

Place the red pepper on a paper towel in the microwave oven and microwave on high for 4 minutes, turning after every minute. Put the pepper in a small bowl, cover with plastic film and leave to cool. Peel off the skin and remove the seeds, then cut out 12 small diamond shapes from the flesh. Set aside.

Put the spinach leaves in a bowl, cover and microwave on high for 4 minutes. Drain the spinach well, taking care not to break up the leaves.

Line the hollows of two plastic egg cartons with plastic film. Divide the sole mixture equally among the 12 moulds and smooth the surface. Divide the spinach leaves into 12 portions and arrange each portion in an even layer over the sole. Top the spinach with an even layer of the salmon mixture. Cook one box at a time on high for 1½ to 2 minutes, until the fish mixtures are just firm to the touch.

Meanwhile, toast the bread and cut out 12 circles with a 4.5 cm (1 ¾ inch) round cutter.

Put a plate over each carton and invert it to remove the fish moulds; drain off any liquid. Lift each mould on to a circle of toast and place a red pepper diamond on top. Arrange the assembled canapés on a plate and serve them warm.

EDITOR'S NOTE: *If you wish to serve the canapés cold, let the fish moulds cool in the egg cartons, then place them on the circles of toast just before serving. Small egg cups may be used in place of plastic egg cartons to cook the fish moulds. The unused sweet pepper may be sliced and used in a salad or puréed for a sauce.*

Peanut and Spinach Pinwheels

Makes 16 pinwheels
Working time: about 20 minutes
Total time: about 1 hour and 20 minutes (includes chilling)

Per pinwheel:
Calories **45**
Protein **3g**
Cholesterol **30mg**
Total fat **3g**
Saturated fat **1g**
Sodium **20mg**

75 g	unsalted roasted peanuts	2 ½ oz
2	eggs	2
30 g	plain flour	1 oz
¼ tsp	salt	¼ tsp
	freshly ground black pepper	
125 g	spinach, stalks removed	4 oz
1 tsp	cornflour	1 tsp
6 tbsp	skimmed milk	6 tbsp
1 tsp	fresh lemon juice	1 tsp
⅛ tsp	grated nutmeg	⅛ tsp

Cut out a 22 cm (9 inch) square of non-stick parchment paper. Fold up the edges to form a shallow lip and place the parchment on a microwave oven tray.

In a food processor, finely grind the peanuts. Break the eggs into a mixing bowl and whisk until thick and frothy. Fold just over half of the peanuts into the eggs along with the flour, salt and a little pepper. Tip the mixture into the prepared parchment and gently spread it into an even layer. Microwave on high for 2 ½ to 3 minutes, turning the tray half a turn after 1 minute. The centre should feel firm to the touch.

Turn out the cooked peanut mixture on to a sheet of non-stick parchment paper, remove the top parchment paper and cover with a new piece of damp non-stick parchment. Roll up like a Swiss roll, with the damp parchment inside, and leave to cool.

Wash the spinach leaves and put them into a casserole dish. Cover and microwave on high for 3 minutes, then drain the spinach well, squeezing out as much water as possible.

In a bowl, mix the cornflour to a paste with a little of the milk, then blend in the remaining milk. Microwave on high for 1 minute, then stir. Chop the spinach and stir it into the sauce. Season with the lemon juice, nutmeg and a little black pepper.

Carefully unroll the roulade and remove the parchment paper. Spread the spinach mixture evenly over the surface, then reroll. Sprinkle the remaining ground peanuts on a piece of greaseproof paper and roll the roulade in them to coat the exterior. Wrap the roulade in greaseproof paper and chill it in the refrigerator for about 1 hour. To serve, remove the paper and cut the roulade into 16 slices.

Leek and Bacon Potatoes

Serves 4
Working time: about 15 minutes
Total time: about 25 minutes

Calories **145**
Protein **8g**
Cholesterol **10mg**
Total fat **2g**
Saturated fat **trace**
Sodium **340mg**

4	potatoes (about 125 g/4 oz each), scrubbed, well, dried and pricked all over with a fork	4
60 g	lean smoked bacon, trimmed of fat and diced	2 oz
125 g	leeks, trimmed, cleaned (page 127) and finely chopped	4 oz
1 tbsp	skimmed milk	1 tbsp
	freshly ground black pepper	

Place the potatoes in a circle on a paper towel in the microwave oven. Cook the potatoes on high for 10 minutes, turning them over after 5 minutes, then remove them from the oven and set them aside.

Put the bacon and leeks into a small bowl and microwave on high for 3 minutes, stirring once.

Cut the tops off the potatoes and scoop out the insides to within 5 mm (¼ inch) of the skins. Mash the scooped-out potato with the milk and season lightly with freshly ground pepper. Stir in the bacon and leeks. Pile the potato, bacon and leek mixture back into the skins, place the lids on top and reheat on high for 1 to 2 minutes before serving.

Glazed Chicken Drumsticks

Makes 6 drumsticks
Working (and total) time: about 30 minutes

Per drumstick:
Calories **130**
Protein **14g**
Cholesterol **25mg**
Total fat **6g**
Saturated fat **2g**
Sodium **115mg**

1 tbsp	honey	1 tbsp
1 tbsp	molasses	1 tbsp
1 tbsp	low-sodium soy sauce or shoyu	1 tbsp
1 tbsp	cider vinegar	1 tbsp
1 tbsp	tomato paste	1 tbsp
1	small garlic clove, crushed	1
1 cm	piece fresh ginger root, peeled and finely chopped	½ inch
3	green cardamom pods, crushed	3
½ tbsp	Dijon mustard	½ tbsp
¼ tsp	salt	¼ tsp
⅛ tsp	cayenne pepper	⅛ tsp
1 tsp	ground arrowroot dissolved in 1 ½ tsp water	1 tsp
6	chicken drumsticks (about 350 g/12 oz), skinned	6
	parsley sprigs, for garnish	

To make the glaze, place all ingredients except the arrowroot, drumsticks and parsley in a bowl, and add 5 tablespoons of water. Microwave on high for 4 minutes, leave to stand for a further 2 minutes, then strain through a fine-meshed sieve, pressing down hard on the spices. Stir in the arrowroot and return the bowl to the oven. Microwave on high for 1 to 1½ minutes, stirring every 20 seconds, until the sweet-and-sour glaze is thick and clear.

Turn the drumsticks in the warm glaze to coat them thoroughly. Arrange in a shallow dish in a wheel-spoke pattern, thin ends to the centre; reserve the glaze. Microwave the drumsticks on high for 2 minutes, then turn them over, and give the dish a quarter turn. Cook for 2 minutes more, then turn over the pieces, give the dish another quarter turn, and pour over the reserved glaze. Reduce the power to low and cook for a further 4 minutes, giving the dish another quarter turn half way through the cooking.

Rest the glazed chicken for 4 minutes, then check for doneness by inserting a thin skewer into the thickest drumstick — the skewer should encounter virtually no resistance. Now grasp the bone and check if it will move slightly within the flesh — if it does, the chicken is cooked. If not cooked through, microwave the drumsticks on medium for a further 2 minutes and rest for 2 more minutes before testing again.

Arrange the drumsticks on a serving plate and spoon the glaze over them. Garnish with the parsley.

EDITOR'S NOTE: *The drumsticks may be left to marinate overnight in the glaze before they are cooked. If you wish to serve them cold, leave them to cool in the glaze.*

Pineapple Chunks Wrapped in Spicy Beef

Makes about 40 chunks
Working time: about 20 minutes
Total time: about 1 hour and 20 minutes
(includes marinating)

Per chunk:	350 g	fillet steak	12 oz
Calories **20**	2 tbsp	sesame oil	2 tbsp
Protein **3g**	2 tbsp	low-sodium soy sauce or shoyu	2 tbsp
Cholesterol **10mg**	1	garlic clove, crushed	1
Total fat **1g**			
Saturated fat **trace**	½ tsp	chili powder	½ tsp
Sodium **5mg**	1	pineapple	1

Slice the steak across the grain as thinly as possible. Cut the slices in half lengthwise, then stretch the pieces with the back of the knife to give strips roughly 7.5 by 1 cm (3 by ½ inch).

Put the oil, soy sauce, garlic and chili powder in a bowl. Stir in the beef slices to coat them well with the sauce. Cover the dish with plastic film and leave the meat to marinate for 1 hour, stirring twice.

Cut the top and bottom off the pineapple. Cut away the skin and slice the flesh into rings about 2 cm (¾ inch) thick. Remove the core from each slice and cut about 40 cubes from the slices.

Wrap a piece of beef round each pineapple chunk and thread on to a cocktail stick. Arrange half of the wrapped chunks on a plate, so that they are evenly spaced round the outside with their sticks pointing towards the centre. Microwave on high for 2 minutes, turning them over gently every 30 seconds. Leave to rest for 5 minutes while you cook the second batch in the same way, then serve.

EDITOR'S NOTE: *The chunks may also be served chilled.*

Vegetable Wholemeal Pizza

Serves 4
Working time: about 25 minutes
Total time: about 45 minutes

Calories **250**
Protein **12g**
Cholesterol **10mg**
Total fat **9g**
Saturated fat **3g**
Sodium **420mg**

¾ tsp	dried yeast	¾ tsp
175 g	wholemeal flour	6 oz
¼ tsp	salt	¼ tsp
15 g	polyunsaturated margarine	½ oz
3	tomatoes, quartered	3
1	small onion, chopped	1
1 tsp	virgin olive oil	1 tsp
	freshly ground black pepper	
1	courgette, sliced	1
5	sweet red pepper rings	5
4	baby sweetcorn	4
60 g	mushrooms, sliced	2 oz
1 tsp	dried oregano	1 tsp
60 g	low-fat mozzarella, grated	2 oz

Reconstitute the dried yeast according to the manufacturer's instructions. Sift the flour and ⅛ teaspoon of the salt into a mixing bowl, adding back the bran from the sieve. Rub in the margarine, then make a well in the centre; pour the yeast into the well and mix it in with a wooden spoon to make a dough that can be formed into a ball.

Turn out the dough on to a lightly floured surface and knead until it is smooth and elastic — 5 to 10 minutes. To prove the dough, put it in a bowl, cover with plastic film and microwave on high for 10 seconds only. Leave to stand for 10 minutes, then microwave on high for a further 10 seconds and leave to rise for 10 minutes; it should double in bulk.

Meanwhile, cook the vegetables. Place the tomatoes on a plate. Microwave on high for 1 to 2 minutes, then remove the skins and chop the flesh. Put the onion in a small bowl with ½ teaspoon of the oil and microwave on high for 2 minutes. Add the tomatoes and season lightly with the remaining salt and a little pepper. Set aside.

Put the courgette, pepper rings, baby sweetcorn and mushrooms in a small bowl with 1 tablespoon of water; cover with plastic film, leaving one corner open, and cook on high for 3 minutes. Drain the vegetables.

Turn the dough out on to a floured surface and knead lightly for 1 minute, then roll it out into a 25 cm (10 inch) circle. Lightly brush a flat 25 cm (10 inch) diameter plate with the remaining oil and place the dough on the plate. Spread the tomato and onion mixture over the dough and arrange the other vegetables over the top of the tomatoes. Sprinkle the oregano and grated mozzarella over the vegetables. Prove the pizza by microwaving it on high for 10 seconds, then resting it for 5 minutes. Cook on high for 5 to 6 minutes. Rest for a further 5 minutes before serving.

Chicken Stock

Makes about 2 litres (3½ pints)
Working time: about 20 minutes
Total time: about 3 hours

2 to 2.5kg	uncooked chicken trimmings and bones (preferably wings, necks and backs), the bones cracked with a heavy knife	4 to 5 lb
2	carrots, cut into 1 cm (½ inch) thick rounds	2
2	sticks celery, cut into 2.5 cm (1 inch) pieces	2
2	large onions, cut in half, one half stuck with 2 cloves	2
2	fresh thyme sprigs, or ½ tsp dried thyme	2
1 or 2	bay leaves	1 or 2
10 to 15	parsley stalks	10 to 15
5	black peppercorns	5

Put the chicken trimmings and bones into a heavy stockpot; pour in enough water to cover them by about 5 cm (2 inches). Bring the liquid to the boil over medium heat, skimming off the scum that rises to the surface. Reduce the heat and simmer the liquid for 10 minutes, skimming and adding a little cold water to help precipitate the scum.

Add the vegetables, herbs and peppercorns, and submerge them in the liquid. If necessary, pour in enough additional water to cover the contents of the pot. Simmer the stock for 2 to 3 hours, skimming as necessary to remove the scum.

Strain the stock and allow it to stand until tepid, then refrigerate it overnight or freeze it long enough for the fat to congeal. Spoon off and discard the layer of fat.

Tightly covered and refrigerated, the stock may safely be kept for three to four days. Stored in small, tightly covered freezer containers and frozen, the stock may be kept for as long as six months.

EDITOR'S NOTE: *The chicken gizzard and heart may be added to the stock. Wings and necks — rich in natural gelatine — produce a particularly gelatinous stock, ideal for sauces and jellied dishes.*

Vegetable Stock

Makes about 2 litres (3½ pints)
Working time: about 25 minutes
Total time: about 1 hour and 30 minutes

4	sticks celery with leaves, cut into 2.5 cm (1 inch) pieces	4
4	carrots, scrubbed and cut into 2.5 cm (1 inch) pieces	4
4	large onions, coarsely chopped	4
3	large broccoli stems, coarsely chopped (optional)	3
1	medium turnip, peeled and cut into 1 cm (½ inch) cubes	1
6	garlic cloves, crushed	6
30 g	parsley leaves and stems, coarsely chopped	1 oz
10	black peppercorns	10
4	fresh thyme sprigs, or 1 tsp dried thyme	4
2	bay leaves	2

Put the celery, carrots, onions, broccoli if you are using it, turnip, garlic, parsley and black peppercorns into a heavy stockpot. Pour in enough cold water to cover the contents by about 5 cm (2 inches). Bring the liquid to the boil over medium heat, skimming off any scum that rises to the surface. When the liquid reaches the boil, stir in the thyme and the bay leaves. Reduce the heat and let the stock simmer undisturbed for 1 hour.

Strain the stock into a large bowl, pressing down lightly on the vegetables to extract all their liquid. Discard the vegetables.

Tightly covered and refrigerated, the stock may safely be kept for five to six days. Stored in small, tightly covered freezer containers and frozen, the stock may be kept for as long as six months.

Fish Stock

Makes about 2 litres (3½ pints)
Working time: about 15 minutes
Total time: about 40 minutes

1 kg	lean fish bones, fins and tails discarded, the bones rinsed thoroughly and cut into large pieces	2 lb
2	onions, thinly sliced	2
2	sticks celery, chopped	2
1	carrot, thinly sliced	1
½ litre	dry white wine	½ litre
2 tbsp	fresh lemon juice	2 tbsp
1	leek, trimmed, split, cleaned (page 127) and sliced (optional)	1
3	garlic cloves, crushed (optional)	3
10	parsley stalks	10
4	fresh thyme sprigs, or 1 tsp dried thyme	4
1	bay leaf	1
5	black peppercorns	5

Put the fish bones, onions, celery, carrot, wine, lemon juice, 2 litres (3½ pints) of cold water, and the leek and garlic cloves if you are using them, in a large, non-reactive stockpot. Bring the liquid to the boil over medium heat, then reduce the heat to maintain a strong simmer. Skim off all the scum that rises to the surface.

Add the parsley, thyme, bay leaf and black peppercorns, and gently simmer the stock for 20 minutes more.

Strain the stock; allow the solids to drain thoroughly before discarding them.

Tightly covered and refrigerated, the fish stock may safely be kept for three days. Stored in small, tightly covered freezer containers and frozen, the stock may be kept for as long as two months.

EDITOR'S NOTE: *Because the bones from oilier fish produce a strong flavour, be sure to use only the bones from lean fish. Sole, plaice, turbot and other flat fish are best. Do not include the fish skin; it could discolour the stock.*

Glossary

Acidulated water: a dilute solution of lemon juice (or vinegar) in water, used to keep certain vegetables from discolouring after they are peeled.

Balsamic vinegar: a mild, intensely fragrant wine-based vinegar made in northern Italy; traditionally it is aged in wooden casks.

Basil: a leafy herb with a strong, spicy aroma when fresh, often used in Italian cooking. Covered with olive oil and refrigerated in a tightly sealed container, fresh basil leaves may be kept for up to six months.

Blanch: to partially cook food by immersing it briefly in boiling water.

Boemboe sesate: an Indonesian ground spice mix containing turmeric, coriander, cumin, galangal and lemon grass. It is available in Asian shops and in some supermarkets.

Bresaola: whole beef fillet, which has been cured in salt and air-dried. It is a speciality of the Lombardy region of Italy and is sold in wafer-thin slices in delicatessen shops.

Brochette: the French name for a skewer; also refers to skewered and grilled meat, fish or vegetables.

Buckwheat flour: a strongly flavoured flour made from roasted buckwheat seeds.

Burghul (also called bulgur): a type of cracked wheat, where the kernels are steamed and dried before being crushed.

Calorie (or kilocalorie): a precise measure of the energy food supplies when it is broken down for use in the body.

Canelle knife: a kitchen utensil used to create small grooves in vegetables for decorative purposes.

Cardamom: the bittersweet, aromatic dried seeds or whole pods of a plant in the ginger family.

Ceps (also called porcini): wild mushrooms with a pungent, earthy flavour that survives drying or long cooking. Dried ceps should be soaked in hot water before they are used.

Chili peppers: A variety of hot or mild red or green peppers. Fresh or dried, most chili peppers contain volatile oils that can irritate the skin and eyes; they must be handled with extreme care (caution, page 18).

Chinese cabbage (also called Chinese leaves): an elongated cabbage resembling cos lettuce, with long broad ribs and crinkled, light green to white leaves.

Chinese five-spice powder: see Five-spice powder.

Cholesterol: a wax-like substance manufactured in the human body and also found in foods of animal origin. Although a certain amount of cholesterol is necessary for proper body functioning, an excess can accumulate in the arteries, contributing to heart disease. See also Monounsaturated fats; Polyunsaturated fats; Saturated fats.

Cloud-ear mushrooms (also called tree ears, tree fungus, mo-er and wood ears): silver-edged, flavourless lichen used primarily for their crunchy texture and dark colour. Sold dried, the mushrooms should be soaked in hot water for 20 minutes before they are used.

Coriander (also called cilantro): the pungent, peppery leaves of the coriander plant or its earthy tasting dried seeds. It is a common seasoning in Middle Eastern, Oriental and Latin-American cookery.

Cottage cheese: a low-fat soft cheese with a mild flavour and a non-uniform texture. It is made from skimmed milk, but the cottage cheese in this book has added cream to give it a fat content of 4 per cent.

Creamed coconut: coconut flesh which has been dried and pressed into blocks.

Crème fraîche: a slightly ripened, sharp-tasting French double cream containing about 35 per cent fat.

Cumin: the aromatic seeds of an umbelliferous plant similar to fennel, used whole or powdered as a spice, especially in Indian and Latin-American dishes. Toasting gives it a nutty flavour.

Curd cheese: any soft cheese made from separated milk curds. The medium-fat curd cheese used in this book contains 12 per cent fat.

Daikon radish (also called mooli): a long, white Japanese radish.

Dark sesame oil (also called Oriental sesame oil): a dark seasoning oil, high in polyunsaturated fats, made from toasted sesame seeds. Because the oil has a relatively low smoking point, it is rarely heated. Dark sesame oil should not be confused or replaced with lighter sesame cooking oils.

Dublin Bay prawn (also called Norway lobster, scampi or langoustine): a large crustacean found in the Atlantic, Mediterranean and Adriatic. The meat, mainly in the tail, is firm and sweet.

Fennel: a herb (also called wild fennel) whose feathery leaves and dried seeds have a mild anise flavour and are much used for flavouring. Its vegetable relative, the bulb — or Florence — fennel (also called finocchio) can be cooked, or eaten raw in salads.

Feta cheese: a salty Greek and Middle Eastern cheese made from goat's or sheep's milk. The curds are ripened in their own salted whey.

Five-spice powder: a pungent blend of ground Sichuan pepper, star anise, cassia, cloves and fennel seeds. It is available in Asian food shops.

Fromage frais: a soft cheese made from skimmed milk. The *fromage frais* used in this book includes a small proportion of added cream and has an 8 per cent fat content.

Galangal: a brown rhizome with white flesh, similar in appearance and taste to ginger. In the West it is more commonly available in its powdered form, which is also known as Laos powder.

Garam masala: an aromatic mixture of ground spices used in Indian cookery. It usually contains coriander, cumin, cloves, ginger and cinnamon. It is available in Asian shops and some supermarkets.

Ginger: the spicy, buff-coloured rhizome, or rootlike stem, of the ginger plant, used as a seasoning either fresh or dried and powdered. Dried ginger makes a poor substitute for fresh ginger root.

Goat cheese: a pungent soft cheese made with goat's milk.

Goujons: small fish or strips of fish which have been coated with crumbs before cooking.

Julienne: the French term for vegetables or other food cut into strips.

Ketjap manis: a dark soy sauce used in Indonesian and Malaysian cooking. It is much sweeter than its Chinese equivalent.

Kumquat: a fruit which resembles a tiny orange, with a thin and edible peel. Kumquats are often used to garnish savoury dishes.

Lamb's lettuce (also called corn salad or mâche): soft tongue-shaped leaves with a nutlike sweetness and underlying astringency.

Lemon grass (citronella): a long, woody, lemon-flavoured stalk that is shaped like a spring onion. Lemon grass is available in Asian shops. To store, refrigerate in plastic film for up to two weeks; lemon grass may also be frozen for storage.

Marjoram: sweet marjoram and its heartier relative pot marjoram are aromatic herbs, related to oregano but milder in flavour.

Mirin: a sweet Japanese cooking wine made from rice. If mirin is unavailable, substitute white wine or sake mixed with an equal amount of sugar.

Monounsaturated fats: one of the three types of fats found in foods. Monounsaturated fats are believed not to raise the level of cholesterol in the blood.

Mozzarella: soft kneaded cheese from southern Italy, traditionally made from buffalo's milk but now also made from cow's milk. Full-fat mozzarella has a fat content of 40 to 50 per cent, but lower-fat versions are available. The low-fat mozzarella used in the recipes in this book has a fat content of only about 16 per cent.

Nam pla: a thin, brown, salty liquid made from fermented fish and used in South East Asian cooking to bring out the flavours of a dish. If not available, substitute a mixture of one part anchovy paste to four parts water.

Non-reactive pan: a cooking vessel whose surface does not chemically react with food. Materials used include stainless steel, enamel, glass and some alloys. Untreated cast iron and aluminium may react with acids, producing discoloration or a peculiar taste.

Nori: paper-like dark green or black sheets of dried seaweed, often used in Japanese cooking as flavouring or as wrappers for rice and vegetables.

Oakleaf lettuce: a delicate red-leafed lettuce.

Olive oil: any of various grades of oil extracted from olives. Extra-virgin olive oil has a full, fruity flavour and very low acidity. Virgin olive oil is lighter in flavour and slightly higher in acidity. Pure olive oil, a processed blend of olive oils, has the lightest taste and highest acidity. For salad dressings, virgin and extra-virgin olive oils are preferred. Store in a cool, dark place.

Peppercorns: the berries of the pepper vine, picked at various stages of ripeness and then dried. Black, white, red and green peppercorns are available.

Pesto: a smooth paste made by pounding basil, garlic, pine-nuts and salt with olive oil. In Italian, *pesto* simply means "pounded".

Phyllo pastry: a paper-thin flour-and-water pastry popular in Greece and the Middle East. It can be bought fresh or frozen from delicatessens and shops specializing in Middle Eastern food.

Pine-nuts: seeds from the cone of the stone pine, a tree native to the Mediterranean. Pine-nuts are used in pesto and other sauces; their buttery flavour can be heightened by light toasting.

Plantain: a green-skinned banana-like fruit, popular in West Indian and African cookery. It must be cooked before it is eaten.

Poach: to cook gently in simmering liquid. The temperature of the poaching liquid should be approximately 94°C (200°F), and its surface should merely tremble.

Polyunsaturated fats: one of the three types of fats found in foods. They exist in abundance in such vegetable oils as safflower, sunflower, corn and soya bean. Polyunsaturated fats lower the level of cholesterol in the blood.

Prosciutto: an uncooked, dry-cured and slightly salt Italian ham, sliced paper-thin.

Punch puran: a mixture in equal proportions of cumin, onion seeds, fennel seeds, fenugreek and mustard seeds. Used in Indian cookery, it is available from Asian food shops.

Quark: a type of soft cheese with a mild, clean, slightly acid flavour. Usually very low in fat, but smoother varieties have added cream. The quark used in this book has a 1 per cent fat content.

Quenelle: a purée of meat or fish, bound with egg whites and cream, then shaped into ovals and poached. Low-fat quenelles can be made using *fromage frais* or yogurt in place of the cream.

Radicchio: a purplish-red Italian chicory with a chewy texture and slightly bitter taste.

Recommended Daily Amount (RDA): the average daily amount of an essential nutrient as recommended for groups of healthy people by the U.K. Department of Health and Social Security.

Red lollo lettuce: a red-tinged, frilly lettuce.

Reduce: to boil down a liquid in order to concentrate its flavour and thicken its consistency.

Rice-paper wrappers: wafer-thin, translucent discs made of rice and water which become supple after a few seconds when dipped in cold water. They are sold in Oriental shops.

Rice vinegar: a mild, fragrant vinegar that is less assertive than cider vinegar or distilled white vinegar. It is available in dark, light, seasoned and sweetened varieties; Japanese rice vinegar is generally milder than the Chinese version.

Ricotta: soft, mild, white Italian cheese, made from cow's or sheep's milk. Full-fat ricotta has a fat content of 20 to 30 per cent, but the low-fat ricotta used in this book has a fat content of only about 8 per cent.

Roe: refers primarily to fish eggs, but edible roe is also found in scallops, crabs and lobsters.

Safflower oil: a vegetable oil that contains a high proportion of polyunsaturated fats.

Saffron: the dried, yellowish-red stigmas (or threads) of the saffron crocus, which yield a powerful yellow colour as well as a pungent flavour. Powdered saffron may be substituted for threads but has less flavour.

Sake: Japanese rice wine. If sake is not available, dry sherry may be substituted.

Sambal oelek: an Indonesian sauce made from chili peppers. Available in Asian shops, sambal oelek makes an excellent substitute for fresh or dried chilies.

Saturated fats: one of the three types of fats found in foods. They exist in abundance in animal products and in coconut and palm oils; they raise the level of cholesterol in the blood. Because high blood-cholesterol levels may cause heart disease, saturated fat consumption should be restricted to less than 15 per cent of the calories provided by the daily diet.

Sauté: to cook a food quickly in a small amount of oil or butter over high heat.

Scallop: a bivalve mollusc found throughout the world, in the Atlantic from Iceland to Spain and in the Pacific from Alaska to Australia. The white nut of meat (actually the adductor muscle) and the orange roe, or coral, are eaten. Tiny queen scallops are a different species from the familiar large scallops known in France as *coquilles Saint-Jacques*.

Sesame oil: see Dark sesame oil.

Sesame seeds: small, nutty-tasting seeds used frequently, either raw or roasted, in Middle Eastern and Indian cookery.

Sherry vinegar: a full-bodied vinegar made from sherry; its distinguishing feature is a sweet aftertaste.

Shiitake mushroom: a variety of mushroom, originally grown only in Japan, available fresh or dried. The dried form should be soaked in hot water for 20 minutes and stemmed before use.

Shoyu: see Soy sauce.

Skimmed milk: milk from which almost all the fat has been removed.

Sodium: a nutrient essential to maintaining the proper balance of fluids in the blood. In most diets, a major source of the element is table salt, made up of 40 per cent sodium. Excess sodium may contribute to high blood pressure, which increases the risk of heart disease. One teaspoon (5.5 g) of salt, with 2,132 milligrams of sodium, contains just over the maximum daily amount recommended by the World Health Organization.

Soured cream: cream that has been thickened by the addition of acid-producing bacteria which give it a tart taste. It has an 18 per cent fat content.

Soy sauce: a savoury, salty brown liquid made from fermented soya beans and available in both light and dark versions. One teaspoon of ordinary soy sauce contains 1,030 milligrams of sodium; lower-sodium variations, such as naturally fermented shoyu, may contain only half that amount. See also Tamari.

Stir-fry: to cook thin slices of vegetables, fish or meat over high heat in a small amount of oil, stirring constantly to ensure even cooking in a short time. The traditional cooking vessel is a Chinese wok; a heavy frying pan may also be used.

Strong flour: a white flour milled from strains of wheat with a high protein content. The high proportion

of protein, which combines with water to form gluten, produces breads with an even texture.

Sushi rice: short-grained Japanese rice which, when cooked, becomes moist, firm and sticky. It is available from Oriental food shops.

Tabasco sauce: a hot, unsweetened chili sauce.

Tahini (also called sesame paste): a nutty-tasting paste made from ground sesame seeds that are usually roasted.

Tamari: a dark, strong-flavoured soy sauce, sometimes described as unfermented or raw soy because of its shorter brewing period.

Tamarillo: a many-seeded fruit, similar to the tomato, but egg-shaped. It can be used in the same way.

Tamarind (also called Indian date): the pulp surrounding the seeds of the tamarind plant, yielding a juice considerably more sour than lemon juice. Grown and used throughout Asia, tamarind is available fresh in pod form, in bricks or as a concentrate.

Tarragon: a strong herb with a sweet anise taste. Because heat intensifies tarragon's flavour, cooked dishes require smaller amounts.

Thyme: a versatile herb with a zesty, slighty fruity flavour and a strong aroma.

Tomato paste: concentrated tomato purée, available in cans and tubes, used in sauces and soups.

Total fat: an individual's daily intake of polyunsaturated, monounsaturated and saturated fats. Nutritionists recommend that fats constitute no more than 35 per cent of a person's total calorie intake. The term as used in the nutrient analyses in this book refers to all the sources of fat in a recipe.

Turmeric: a yellow spice from a plant related to ginger, used as a colouring agent and occasionally as a substitute for saffron. Turmeric has a musty odour and a slightly bitter flavour.

Wakame: a seaweed used in Japanese cooking. Bought in dried form, it must be soaked in tepid water for 20 minutes before use.

Wasabi: a Japanese horseradish, usually sold in powdered form. The powder is mixed with water to form a fiery green paste, which is then served with sushi or noodles.

Wholemeal flour: wheat flour which contains the whole of the wheat grain with nothing added or taken away. It is nutritionally valuable as a source of dietary fibre and is higher in B vitamins than white flour.

Wild rice: the seed of a water grass native to the Great Lakes region of the United States. It is appreciated for its nutty flavour and chewy texture.

Wonton wrapper: a thin dough wrapper, about 9 cm (3½ inches) square, made of wheat flour and egg and used to encase spicy fillings of meat, fish or vegetables.

Index

Picture Credits

Cover: Chris Knaggs. 4: top, James Murphy; bottom left, Chris Knaggs; bottom right, John Elliott. 5: top, left and right, James Murphy; bottom, Chris Knaggs. 6: Chris Knaggs. 10: Ian O'Leary. 12-13: Martin Brigdale. 14-17: Philip Modica. 18-21: James Murphy. 22: top, Philip Modica; bottom, Taran Z. Photography. 23: Chris Knaggs. 24: Simon Butcher. 25: top, James Murphy; bottom, Chris Knaggs. 27-28: John Elliott. 29: James Murphy. 30-31: John Elliott. 32: Chris Knaggs. 33: John Elliott. 34: Jan Baldwin. 35: James Murphy. 36-39: Chris Knaggs. 40: John Elliott. 41: Andrew Whittuck. 42-45: John Elliott. 46: Philip Modica. 47-48; John Elliott. 49: Chris Knaggs. 50-53: Jan Baldwin. 54-56: Chris Knaggs. 57: Andrew Whittuck. 58: Chris Knaggs. 59: Philip Modica. 60: Jan Baldwin. 61: Chris Knaggs. 62: Jan Baldwin. 63-64: John Elliott. 65: Chris Knaggs. 66: top, Jan Baldwin; bottom, John Elliott. 67: Jan Baldwin. 68-69: John Elliott. 70: Philip Modica. 71: Chris Knaggs. 72: Andrew Whittuck. 73: Philip Modica. 74-75: John Elliott. 76: top, John Elliott; middle and bottom, Taran Z. Photography. 77: John Elliott. 78: Jan Baldwin. 79: Chris Knaggs. 80: John Elliott. 81: Chris Knaggs. 82: Philip Modica. 83: David Johnson. 84: John Elliott. 85: Andrew Whittuck. 86-88: Chris Knaggs. 89: John Elliott. 90: Andrew Whittuck. 91: Chris Knaggs. 92-94: John Elliott. 95: Jan Baldwin. 96: Andrew Whittuck. 97: Philip Modica. 98: top, John Elliott; bottom, Andrew Whittuck. 99: Philip Modica. 100-101: Jan Baldwin. 102-103: Chris Knaggs. 104-105: James Murphy. 106: John Elliott. 107-111: James Murphy. 112-113: Chris Knaggs. 114: James Murphy. 115-116: Chris Knaggs. 117: James Murphy. 118: John Elliott. 119: James Murphy. 120: top, James Murphy; bottom, Renée Comet. 121-122: Chris Knaggs. 123: Martin Brigdale. 124: Jan Baldwin. 125: Chris Knaggs. 126: John Elliott. 127: top, Chris Knaggs; bottom, Taran Z. Photography. 128-138: John Elliott.

Props: The editors wish to thank the following outlets and manufacturers; all are based in London unless otherwise stated. 4: top: china, Fortnum & Mason; 5: top: plate, Hutschenreuther (U.K.) Ltd.; fork, Mappin & Webb Silversmiths; bottom: plate, Villeroy & Boch; 6: china, Hutschenreuther (U.K.) Ltd.; 14 top: plate, Rosenthal (London) Ltd.; bottom: bowl, Royal Copenhagen Porcelain and Georg Jensen Silversmiths Ltd.; 15: plate, Hutschenreuther (U.K.) Ltd.; 16: top: bowl, Rosenthal (London) Ltd.; 17: plate, Rosenthal (London) Ltd.; 18: bowl, Royal Copenhagen Porcelain and Georg Jensen Silversmiths Ltd.; 19: china, Fortnum & Mason; 23: china, Fortnum & Mason; lace cloth, Laura Ashley; 25: bottom: platter, Royal Worcester, Worcester; 30: plates, Hutschenreuther (U.K.) Ltd.; 33: plate, Rosenthal (London) Ltd.; Formica, Newcastle, Tyne and Wear; 34: tablecloth, Osborne & Little plc; 36: tablecloth, Ewart Liddell; 37: china, Hutschenreuther (U.K.) Ltd.; 39: plate, Rosenthal (London) Ltd.; 42: plates, The Mid Wales Development Centre; 46: marble, W. E. Grant & Co. (Marble) Ltd.; 48: pottery, Winchcombe Pottery, The Craftsmen Potters Shop; 50: silver, Mappin & Webb Silversmiths; glasses, Kilkenny; 54-55: pottery, Tony Gant, The Craftsmen Potters Shop; 56: top: napkin, Kilkenny; 58: carpet and plates, Persian Rugs Gallery Ltd.; 59: plates, Spode, Worcester; 66: top: pottery, Clive Bowen, The Craftsmen Potters Shop; 67: china, Hutschenreuther (U.K.) Ltd.; 75: plate, Rosenthal (London) Ltd.; 77: lace cloth, Laura Ashley; 80: plate, Royal Worcester, Worcester; candelabra, Mappin & Webb Silversmiths; 83: plate, Rosenthal; 85: plate, Hutschenreuther (U.K.) Ltd.; 87: china, Fortnum & Mason; 90: platter, Royal Worcester, Worcester; 98: pottery, Winchcombe Pottery, The Craftsmen Potters Shop; 100: plate, Royal Worcester, Worcester; 104: china, Spode, Worcester; cutlery, Mappin & Webb Silversmiths; 105: china, Hutschenreuther (U.K.) Ltd.; spoon, Mappin & Webb Silversmiths; 109: china, Hutschenreuther (U.K.) Ltd.; fork, Mappin & Webb Silversmiths; cloth, Ewart Liddell; 110-111: plates, Royal Worcester, Worcester; 114: plate, Hutschenreuther (U.K.) Ltd.; 118: cutlery, Mappin & Webb Silversmiths; 121: plate, Villeroy & Boch; 123: napkin, Kilkenny; 126: plate, Royal Worcester, Worcester; napkin, Ewart Liddell; 127: top: plate, Micky Doherty, The Craftsmen Potters Shop; 128: marble, W. E. Grant & Co. (Marble) Ltd.; 134: china, Chinacraft Ltd.; 135: plates, Villeroy & Boch; 138: flour jar, Andrew and Jane Young, The Craftsmen Potters Shop.

Acknowledgements

The index for this book was prepared by Myra Clark. The editors wish to thank: Paul van Biene, London; René Bloom, London; Maureen Burrows, London; Stuart Cullen, London; Jonathan Driver, London; Molly Hodgson, Richmond, Yorkshire; Irena Hoare, London; Lawleys, London; Line of Scandinavia, London; Next Interiors, London; Christine Noble, London; Oneida, London; Elisabeth Lambert Ortiz, London; Perstorp Warerite Ltd., London; Katherine Reeve, London; Sharp Electronics (U.K.) Ltd., London; Jane Stevenson, London; Toshiba (U.K.) Ltd., London.

Colour Separations by Fotolitomec, S.N.C., Milan, Italy
Typesetting by G. Beard & Son Ltd., Brighton, Sussex, England
Printed and bound by Brepols S.A., Turnhout, Belgium